A Layma

at the History, Industry, People

and Places of

Oughtibridge, Worrall and

Wharncliffe Side

BY

DOUG SANDERSON

ACKNOWLEDGMENTS

Whilst most of the information contained in the book is from my own memories and knowledge accumulated over the years, I would like to thank all the people who have contributed in any way to the publication.

The Bradfield Parish Council; M Nunn, G.V.Stanley, E Goddard, J. Ambler,
E Glossop, P Clarke, A Clarke, J Swift,
The Rev'd. Canon Lewis Atkinson and T Nicholson.

© Doug Sanderson 1999
Second Edition 2001

ISBN 1-901587-15-0

Published & Printed by:
ALD Design & Print
279 Sharrow Vale Road
Sheffield S11 7ZF
0114 267 9402

INTRODUCTION

The history of Sheffield as a centre for steel-making is a fascinating story of human vision and endeavour spread over the last two hundred years. The ready availability of nature's resources such as ganister, coal and clay and of course, water, resulted in many small family businesses emerging, often connected with file making or the cutlery industry, working as 'Little Mesters'.

There are many local stories to tell and Doug Sanderson, with his local knowledge of Oughtibridge, Worrall and Wharncliffe Side, brings many to life in his book. It is not only about the rise and fall of industry in the area, but also about the effects on communities, the buildings and the people.

It is a privilege to write this introduction to Doug's book which I recommend to you.

Canon Lewis Atkinson, Vicar.   October 1999

CONTENTS

Chapter

1   EARLY HISTORY.

2   OUR INDUSTRIAL HERITAGE.

         [i]   Iron and Steel.
         [ii]   Quarrying.
         [iii]   Mining.
         [iv]   Refractory.
         [v]   Paper.
         [vi]   Other Industry.

3   BUILDINGS, PLACES AND PEOPLE.
         [i]   Hayward's.
         [ii]   The Inns.
         [iii]   Churches.
         [iv]   Schools.
         [v]   Shops.
         [vi]   Other Buildings.

4   WADSLEY - A NEIGHBOUR OF DISTINCTION.

5   PLACE NAMES.

6   VILLAGE CRICKET.

7   VILLAGE FOOTBALL.

8   THE VILLAGE BAND.

9   PASTIMES.

10   CHORES OF DAYS PAST.

11   YESTERDAYS TREATS AND CURES.

FOREWORD

With the decline of our industries, this area has increasingly become a dormitory for people commuting to Sheffield and other parts of South Yorkshire. Many of the new residents are unaware of the history of the district but are eager for information about the people, industry and buildings. For many years the writer has taken an interest in local history and, when talking to people, has frequently been asked if the information has been written down. This book is a direct result of these inquiries and, as the author was born into an old and well known local family, much of the information stems from his own personal knowledge and experience, from other old residents, historical records and Census returns.

Considerable efforts have been made to ensure the veracity of the information contained in the book, which is not intended to be an historical work, but rather an insight into the way of life of people in the area as well as a brief look at our history.

A LOOK AT THE HISTORY, INDUSTRY, BUILDINGS AND PEOPLE OF OUGHTIBRIDGE, WHARNCLIFFE SIDE AND WORRALL

EARLY HISTORY

Our story began in the shadowy days of pre-history with the finding in 1873 of the fossilized remains of tree stumps in the grounds of what was then the South Yorkshire Lunatic Asylum. Dating back to the Carboniferous Age, some two hundred and fifty million years ago, these can still be seen in the grounds of the old Middlewood Hospital. Any development that takes place there will have to accommodate the preservation of this ancient site.

Millions of years later, primitive man came with his flint weapons and around ten thousand years ago lived by hunting on the moors of Bradfield and Wharncliffe. Their settlements, of which little trace remains, were primitive indeed, as they neither tilled the land or kept flocks, relying on the rivers for fish, animals for meat and nature for the fruits of the earth.

With the coming of the Romans, the early Britons were taught the art of social life and Agricola and his successors encouraged their veteran soldiers to stay in Britain and marry local women. With Roman encampments at Templeborough and Brough and over the Pennines at Dinting, it is likely to have taken place in this area.

Centuries later, before the Norman invasion, evidence suggests that the feudal system existed as early records mention Manors at Worrall, Ughill and Wadsley, held by Aldene. He was shown to hold fourteen bovates of land, two ploughs and a pasturable wood, a mile square. A bovate of land being as much land as could be ploughed by one Ox in one year.

After the Conquest, Waltheof, the last of the Saxon Lords, retained Hallam until he was executed in 1076 for conspiring against William the Conqueror. His estates passed to his wife, the daughter of William's sister, Adeliza, and the Manors of Ughill, Worrall and Wadsley were held under her by Roger de Busli, the first Norman Lord of Hallamshire, who's estate later became known as the Honor of Blythe.

Early records have few references to Oughtibridge although it was mentioned in a record dated 1161. Even as late as 1747 it consisted of only five families. Worrall or Wirrall was mentioned in an agreement of 1294 when Robert de Wadsley granted certain lands at Wirrall to Robert, son of Nicholas de Langers, for the sum of four shillings and one penny, in silver. In 1297, Thomas de Furnival granted a Charter to the men of Wadsley and Worrall, allowing them to graze cattle and collect wood, "betwixt the rivulet of Onesacre and the road leading to Bradfield, and between Uggibroke and Langcetcliffe".

In 1481, Richard Everingham and his wife, Agnes, were granted a license to have

Mass celebrated in their presence in any Chapel or Oratory within the manors of Oghtibrigge and Waddesley.

In a Charter dated 1541, Henry Everingham, Lord of the manors of Worrall and Wadsley, granted reliefs to the freeholders and their heirs in these manors, for ever, from paying reliefs, wrongful duties and other customs, provided they attended court and paid a fealty and then paid their yearly rent.

A later Henry Everingham, whose fortunes were deteriorating, conveyed the manor of Worrall to Robert Swyft Esq. in 1557. His son, also named Robert, had no sons and the manors of Wadsley, Worrall and Wickersly passed to Frances, his youngest daughter, in a deed dated 22 September 1561. Sir Francis Leake, husband of Frances conveyed the manors of Wadsley and Worrall to George, sixth Earl of Shrewsbury, the paramount Lord at Sheffield Castle who died seized of them in 1590, as did his son, Gilbert, the Seventh Earl, in 1616. They were listed among the possessions of the family in the great entail of 3 Charles 1, the entail being created to list the possessions of an estate which were to settle on a series of heirs, so that the immediate possessor may not dispose of the estate.

Over the years, Worrall and the surrounding area was closely associated with Wadsley which had developed as an important centre of the cutlery trade and became famous for the manufacture of pocket knives.

OUR INDUSTRIAL HERITAGE

IRON AND STEEL

As far back as the 17th Century some industry existed locally, but only Wortley Top Forge has survived to provide a splendid example of the skill and ingenuity of the craftsmen who, in the last century, working with primitive tilt hammers, forged railway axles that no doubt were used on railways throughout the world. The renovated site at Wortley and the restored machinery, including the water powered tilt hammer, provide us with a glimpse of Britain's past when our industry supplied much of the worlds goods.

During the later part of the 18th and in the 19th centuries the population expanded rapidly, much of it to do with farming and the cutlery industry, but even more due to the industrial revolution and the development of Sheffield as a centre for steel making. This was due to the invention by Benjamin Huntsman in the 1740's of the crucible process for making steel, and to the discovery of a method of plating a copper ingot with silver, which led to the rapid expansion of the silverware and Sheffield plate industry.

Before the Industrial Revolution, the population of Sheffield was around forty thousand and the present suburbs were isolated villages. Places like Darnall, Ecclesfield and Dore and Totley were almost self supporting communities. In this area, Wadsley had already become well known for the manufacture of pocket knives and had an influence on the surrounding district. People and traders from the north would have difficulty approaching the village until the bridge for Wadsley was built over the Don, that area later becoming the village of Wadsley Bridge. In 1841 the population of what we now refer to as Oughtibridge was recorded as 1005 and by 1891, fifty years later, it had grown to 1784. From an examination of Census returns, we find that many of the families were large with ten or more children being commonplace, no doubt necessary with the high mortality rate of the time. Many of the households were shown as having lodgers, whilst daughters were employed as Domestic Servants or working in shops, pubs or at the Paper Mill. Although many of the men were working in the File and Cutlery trades, others were working in a variety of industries including mining, brickmaking, steel forging, quarrying, stone mason and spindle making.

The people living in the isolated cottages and farms in Worrall, Loxley and Oughtibridge with their 'Little Mester' workshops, would no doubt find it easier to trade with Wadsley, rather than travel the much longer distance to Sheffield. In later years, many of these workshops were associated with the file trade rather than the cutlery industry and, sadly, very few of them have survived so we have to rely on old records and census returns to remind us of their existence. Two definitions of what constituted a Little Mester seem to exist. One would involve him in collecting the knife or file blanks from the larger manufacturer, usually in Sheffield and, after agreeing a price for the job, employing others to perform the work at the lowest wage possible. This often resulted in desperately low income for some. The finished goods were returned on the following Monday morning, often being transported by pony and cart or carried over the shoulder. The lower the wages the more profit for the Little Mester. The other description would portray him as a truly skilled man who could perform all the operations necessary in the manufacture of the finished product. This particularly applied to the cutlery industry and the manufacture of pocket knives where, as automation replaced hand manufacture and many of our cutlery manufacturers ceased production, more and more of the Little Mesters went out of business. Today, very few exist but one or two continue to demonstrate their skills in local industrial museums. One gentleman, Stan Shaw, who was born in Worrall and is a true "Little Mester", remains in business making superior quality hand made pocket knives for those who wish to have a reminder of a product which made Sheffield famous.

Although most of the industrial expansion took place in Sheffield, the surrounding district also saw new factories, forges and workshops being built. The new industries required power and the nearest and cheapest source of power was water. All along the tributaries of the Don the remains of this industrialization can still be seen, although only at Abbeydale Industrial Hamlet and Shepherds Wheel have things survived intact. Together with the valleys of the Porter, Sheaf, Loxley and Rivelin, the Don valley had its new industries, with Steel Works at Wardsend, Niagara Works at Wadsley Bridge and Clay Wheel Works along Clay Wheel Lane starting manufacture.

Nearer to Oughtibridge at what was known as Hangman, with its Monkey Rack walk for courting couples, was the Beely Wood Works. For many years the works were referred to as 'Darwin's', who owned the rolling mills there. Opposite the bottom of Beely Road was Middlewood Iron Works, owned by Kenyons, and later the Blackwell family. For some time the chimney remained as the last reminder of its industrial past, before being demolished to allow the site to be developed. Old photographs show cottages in the works, one of which required the occupants to go outside and up a stone staircase in order to go to bed. A little nearer to the centre of Oughtibridge is Forge Hill. By its name one would expect to find a forge there, and on the left was Middlewood Forge and Tilt with its dam providing water for the works. The dam, now filled in and used as a transport company site, drew its water from the Don via a culvert near to the bridge. After servicing the works, the water was put back into the river by means of another culvert under Low Road which until recently could be seen from the footpath alongside the sports field. The entrance to the culvert was sealed at the time that the new sewer was constructed under the river Don.

In the centre of the village is Forge Lane with its reminders of what must have been amongst the earliest of the districts industries. At the entrance are the two stone gate posts on which large wrought iron gates bearing the Wharncliffe crest once hung. Evidence suggests that as far back as 1603 there was a goyt there drawing water from the Don to serve the industry along the lane. Records show that there was a Tannery there in 1644 and that George Hall, who was a Malster, had buildings there around 1700, whilst the Corn Mill was run by George Grayson who married the granddaughter of Henry Hall in 1776.

The forge, a listed building, which still stands, is rapidly falling into a ruinous state due to neglect and vandalism. Whether it was built in 1792 by George Grayson or his son-in-law, John Bedford of More Hall is not known but the Bedford family became prominent industrialists in Sheffield for many years and also left their mark in Oughtibridge with Bedford Road, Bedford Square and Bedford House Farm bearing their name. Bedford House Farm was part of The Oughtibridge Comrades Club until its closure. John Bedford of Wadsley was one of the Committee of Management of Worrall National School when it was opened in 1848.

By 1861 the forge was being run by John Wood who lived in Broomfield House, a large stone built dwelling two hundred yards from the forge at the bottom of Bedford Road. In 1841 he was described as a Journeyman Forger who lived there with his wife Martha and one year old daughter, Elizabeth. Ten years later in 1851 he was a Master Forger employing two men, whilst by 1861 it would appear that he had married Elizabeth Blackwell and had a twelve year old step-son, Arthur Blackwell, living with him. Eventually, in 1884, Arthur took over the forge and later acquired Middlewood Iron Works. To the residents of Oughtibridge, the sound of the steam hammers of Arthur Blackwell and Son Ltd., working night and day throughout the first half of this century, was a constant reminder of the industrial nature of the area.

Further up the valley at Wharncliffe Side was another small steel works alongside the Don at Dyson Holmes, known as Holmes Works. Nothing remains of the works except a few of the large stone retaining walls and the traces of the goyt that drew water from the Don several hundred yards up the valley. Tilt Cottage, a few yards from the works, is still occupied and has an interesting feature in that it has a recess in the wall through which, in days gone by, the workers were handed their pay. The closure of the works in the 1920's brought to an end some two hundred years of industry. Higher up the valley at Stocksbridge, Samuel Fox, who lived at Hathersage, started his umbrella frame manufacturing company which eventually became the mighty Samuel Fox Ltd which was nationalised and became part of British Steel. Of all the steel companies in the area only this has survived to the present day as part of United Engineering Steels.

In Oughtibridge, two other steel companies existed which did not rely on the Don as a source of power. Up Station Lane immediately above the railway line was the entrance to Wardlow's steel works, which for many years bore the Dragon of Wharncliffe crest. This has been moved to the Bradfield Parish Council premises. Water for the works was supplied by Wardlow's Dam which was the scene of a fatality. During hot summer weather, some of the workers made a practice of eating lunch, seated beside the dam and would often finish by having a quick dip in the water before returning to work. On one occasion a swimmer became trapped in some underwater obstacle and was drowned. Higher up the hillside, the Rabok works started out as a steel works but later became better known for the manufacture of rouge polishing wool for the silverware industry. The ladies of the district who worked there, could always be recognised by their rouge coloured complexions.

The last of the companies associated with steel was a hand tool manufacturer with premises along Forge Lane. In 1905 the Co-operative Sheep Shear was formed to manufacture spring handled shears which were exported to many sheep rearing countries throughout the world. For many years there was hardly a house in the area without a pair of shears which had been made at the co-operative and which were used to cut grass by hand, before the development of the lawn mower. With the introduction of the electric motor, the market for spring shears diminished and production eventually ceased although, many years later, at the end of the century, they were still being produced by Burgin and Ball Ltd. on Holme Lane.

Blackwells Forge in former times

Blackwells Forge 1999

Middlewood Iron Works now demolished

Wagtail Wheel Corn Mill - Wheel Lane, Oughtibridge

Charles Bramall

The Yews - Home of the Bramall's, Worrall

QUARRYING

Before the Industrial Revolution the population in the area was still very small and consisted mainly of farmers and agricultural workers. During the seventeenth century more and more people began farming so that many of the farm houses of today with their uniform type of construction, can be dated from 1650 onwards,. Hamlets and other small communities were created, giving rise to a big demand for stone for the farms and cottages of the agricultural workers. This demand led to a rapid expansion of quarrying.

Throughout the area, from the Canyard Hills to Wadsley Common, the remains of the old quarry sites can be seen in the Delphs, Hagg Stones, Low Ash, Onesmoor, The Foldrings, and many other places. In more recent times other sites were being quarried, near to Church Street in Oughtibridge and at the bottom of Langsett Avenue, whilst at Middlewood Quarry, owned by Joseph Turner who lived at Sycamore House, Worrall, stone was being extracted, some of which was used for the construction of the Wicker Arches and other buildings in Sheffield. Quarrying continued there until the last war when the premises were taken over by the Ministry of Defence and used as testing ground for armour plated steel sheets and ammunition. The re-enforced concrete buildings and underground storage places can still be seen.

THE MINING INDUSTRY

The growth of the steel industry led to another activity in the district which was to last for many years until it ceased around 1950. Some two hundred years ago, the area had been extensively surveyed as to what minerals there may be and, although the survey did not show that any of the rarer minerals were present, three were there in abundance, clay, coal and ganister. Many people express doubts when asked about ganister, which is a quartz like crystalline sedimentary rock, similar to sandstone, but with a finer grain and which has two properties that make it very useful in industry. Being able to withstand very high temperatures and having a low level of impurities, it was ideal for use as a lining material in furnaces and kilns and as a material for making the moulds used in the manufacture of steel ingots.

During the nineteenth century, farming was often a hard and unrewarding way of life and farmers would seize any opportunity to supplement their income, especially during the winter months when work on the farm was restricted by the weather. An examination of old Census returns often recorded a farmer as 'Farmer and Filecutter', or 'Farmer and Cutler'. One such farmer, Joseph Bramall, born in 1807 was by 1850 married and living at Birtin Farm along Birtin Lane, at Oughtibridge, and was listed as a file cutter and farmer. He noticed that outcroppings of stone on his farm were somewhat different to the rest, and after investigation it proved to be Ganister. Mining in an area near to the Yews, he later started mining at what was to become Langhouse Colliery, an opencast quarry site along Long Lane near to Lang House at Worrall. Nothing remains to remind us of the work carried out there, as the site was used as a repository for all the road surface material excavated during the installation of Supertram track in Sheffield. The area has now been landscaped, hiding for ever this piece of our industrial history.

By 1871 Joseph Bramall, his wife Elizabeth and three sons had taken up residence at Lang House. Encouraged by the increasing demand for Ganister based furnace lining materials as the number of industrial concerns grew, the Bramalls began Drift mining in the fields between Lang House and Stubbing Lane at Worrall. Very little remains to remind us of the extensive mining carried out there, as the land has been returned to agricultural use and is now flat, with no signs of subsidence from collapsed workings. Mining maps show how intensively the area was worked, with seams extending in all directions, leaving Stubbing Farm on an island of un-mined ground. Reminders of all the work that took place in that locality can be seen across Long Lane on ground that is now part of Hillsborough Golf Club. The remains of the spoil heaps and the cutting that carried the tramway across the Golf Course can be seen. The drift mines passed under Long Lane and it is said that a miner was killed when the road collapsed as he was passing under it with tramway trucks, or corves as they were known. This seems possible as, in 1997, the road collapsed at this point revealing the underground mine workings. Mining maps show a second drift crossing under the road only a few yards away, so perhaps another hole can be expected to appear one day. A short distance

Buffalo on Wharncliffe Chase

Toll Bar Cottage - Cockshutts Lane
With Telephone No. 1 Line to P Dixon & Son Ltd

along Long Lane another tramway crossed the road, and the site of the engine house which powered the cable used in pulling the corves can still be seen. The Bramalls no doubt realised that more money could be made by selling the finished products rather than the extracted ganister, and this resulted in them starting their own factory on what is now the golf course. Old Ordnance Survey maps show the site, which Bramall's called Caledonian Works, some hundreds of yards up on the golf course, towards what was known as Bull Piece, an area of ground where the sport of bull baiting took place in days gone by and where mining had already taken place.

Entrance to the works can still be seen on Worrall Road, alongside the access road to the Golf Club at the top of the Sough Dyke. A new five barred gate stands at the entrance to the works, although the mature trees growing on the access road give an indication of how many years have passed since it was in use. Crushing plant was installed and kilns built and the ore was crushed and ground limestone added to form what was known as 'Pug'. This could be sold as a furnace lining material or hand moulded into bricks which were baked in the kilns, using the coal extracted as a by-product in the mining for the ganister. A great deal of coal must have been obtained in this way, as the Bramalls owned a coal distribution business which, together with their mining, ganister and farming interests, must have made them one of the major employers of labour in the district. As a reminder of the extent of all the mining that took place, a Ganister crushing machine can be seen alongside the entrance to the Kelham Island Museum. Charles Bramall was made an Alderman and lived with his family in The Yews, the large house at Worrall, later used by the Trent Regional Health Authority. The business ceased trading in 1925. In 1891, the Census return showed him as living in Quarry Cottage at Worrall, with Joseph Bramall living at Willow Farm, registered as a Coal and Ganister Merchant.

The Bramalls were not alone in mining for ganister which was taking place over a wide area. Other families were similarly engaged. George Longden and Sons Ltd. were operating at the Bower Mine at Wadsley, whilst William Siddons was mining on Wadsley Common and at the opencast quarry site at Studfield Hill. This was in fact the last site where ganister mining took place until it ceased around 1950. The site has now been landscaped. At Deepcar, Lowoods were mining under Wharncliffe Crags, whilst the Brookes family, who came from Huddersfield and owned The Oughtibridge Silica Firebrick Company Ltd., were busy mining in Wharncliffe woods.

Mining had been carried out there by Beaumonts as early as 1865 in an area known as Oughtibridge Hagg, but the Silica workings extended much further in their Woodend mine, until the last war. In Beely Woods extensive mining was carried out in order to provide the large amounts of minerals required by the company. The old mining maps show the seams and excavations so close together that, as a column of ganister with its associated coal seam was left every few feet to act as a roof support, it must have resembled an underground car park. A walk in Beely Woods still reveals relics of this mining age, with collapsed mine workings and pieces of tramway and wheels from trucks, lying in the undergrowth. By 1920 most of the mining had ceased, with The Asplands mine at Hagg Stones and the Hope Mine below Middlewood Quarry already closed. Work carried on at the Myers clay pit during the 1930's, providing work for one or two men, extracting clay for Oughtibridge Silica Works. For many years the chute alongside the road at Usher Wood was a well know landmark and the three sided stone walled recess where the wagons were loaded, still remain as a reminder of the work carried on there.

Although mining provided much needed work for many people over several decades, it was not without cost to the workers, especially those working in the drift mines. Conditions below ground were unpleasant, with men working in damp and difficult conditions, lying on their side and working by the light of a few candles as they picked at the work face. This was often loosened by the use of explosives, leaving the atmosphere thick with dust, which, as time passed gradually encrusted the lungs of the men, causing them to contract the dreaded silicosis. Lucky were the families who escaped without having to watch a loved one slowly die or suffer from the disease.

The extent of the mining in the area is hard to imagine, with hillsides honeycombed with workings. Mining maps show the extent of most of the workings but fail to show many of the earlier mines. An example of this was seen when excavations for the foundations of the houses on the Grange Farm estate at Worrall were started. The underground mine workings found a few feet below the surface, approximately four to five feet in height, were brick lined and appeared to be in as good a condition as the day they were built, perhaps early in the nineteenth century.

Ganister had another use in earlier times as a road surface material for filling pot-holes before the introduction of Tar-Macadam.

THE REFRACTORY INDUSTRY

Mention has already been made of Oughtibridge Silica Firebrick Company Ltd. whose premises were up Station Lane at Oughtibridge. The site above the railway line adjoining Wharncliffe woods was known as The Top Yard and the other, below the railway on the opposite side of Station Lane, was known as The Bottom Yard. For many years the company was a major employer of labour in the area and remained as a private company until the business was acquired by the Steetley Company Ltd., who continued to operate for several years. With changing market conditions, business operations were gradually reduced and the Bottom Yard, which had its own railway siding along Station Lane, was closed, to be followed some time later by the Top Yard. The Bottom Yard site has recently been developed and is now a housing estate.

Over several decades the company had been a mainstay of village life, supporting local organisations and acting as local benefactors. The General Manager, Edwin Halstead was one of the founder members of the village band when it was formed in the last century, whilst the ground belonging to the village sports club was donated by the company in 1922, as a War Memorial to the fallen of the Great War of 1914-1918. The closure of the company marked the passing of yet another of the industries in the area, but in the neighbouring Loxley valley, where the good quality 'Stannington Clay' had no doubt encouraged the Wragg, Lomas, Marshall and Dyson families to start their refractory works, business was to continue until the end of the century.

Another company busy making bricks was situated at the bottom of Langsett Avenue at Middlewood. Owned by Daniel Doncaster and Co. Ltd., a name more closely associated with steel, the bricks made there could always be recognised by the D◇D mark, whilst up the valley at Deepcar, Lowoods had their factory.

Up Cockshutts Lane, or Jossey Lane as it was known for many years, was a pottery works where, among other things, repute has it that a large tea-pot capable of holding twenty cups of tea was once made. Just where it was located is open to conjecture as old maps would appear to place it on the right hand side of the road near to where Broomfield Terrace now stands. I had always assumed that the small dam on the opposite side of the road, known as Crapper's Pond, which provided many hours of fun for children catching frog spawn and minnows during the school holidays, was part of the works. One of the main products manufactured there would appear to have been clay pipes which were in common use by the working class. In 1881 Tom Sanderson was employed as a Clay Pipe Dresser at the works.

Station Road c1930 with Oughtibridge Silica Firebrick Co. Ltd

Steam Lorry. Peter Dixon & Son Ltd

PAPER MANUFACTURING

Sadly, so many of our local industries have been consigned to history and only one has survived and is still busy manufacturing. For almost one hundred and fifty years, paper has been produced at Wharncliffe Side, and to older people, is synonymous with the Dixon family.

Although a Yorkshire family, originating from around Batley, before moving to Oughtibridge, Mr. Peter Dixon was in business in Glasgow as a rag and paper merchant and also owned a paper mill in Fifeshire. A customer of theirs, T & J Marsh Ltd. who owned a small paper mill at Oughtibridge, was anxious to sell the business, which was losing money. Twenty years earlier in 1851, T. & J. Marsh had taken over a building which, since 1834 had been used for the manufacture of gun cotton, and had installed paper making machinery. The basic raw material for paper at that time was rags, but the quality left much to be desired, so that when the machinery became unreliable, the company became un-economic. The Dixon's bought the premises for £8500, repaired the faulty machinery, introduced new equipment and the company of Peter Dixon and Son Ltd., Spring Grove Works came into being. Mr. Peter Dixon put his son Joseph in charge, although at the time he was only 22 years of age. This was a wise move as Joseph proved to be a shrewd and careful man and over the next years transformed a small mill producing brown paper, into a company with eight machines producing newsprint and which had extensive interests in other fields. In those early days Joseph lived at Dyson Holmes where he was later joined by his father, Peter. In 1873, shortly after his marriage, Joseph built the family home at Spring Grove, Wharncliffe Side, on the hillside overlooking the mill, and lived there until his death in 1926.

In 1872 the company bought six tons of woodpulp in order to try and find an alternative to rags as the major raw material and so became amongst the first newsprint manufacturers to use this new medium. With the passing years, the company prospered and became known as producers of the best quality newsprint. On several occasions they were leaders in the field and introduced innovative ideas, but all was not smooth running. In 1892 a serious fire took place, but luckily much of the equipment was saved. This was followed in 1899 by a much more serious incident when a fire caused damage which resulted in an insurance claim of £14820. At that time Oughtibridge was outside the city limits and with the primitive telephone system of those days, it took some time to contact the Fire Station. The Fire Officer considered it did not warrant sending the steam engine and sent a horse drawn appliance instead. This took some time to get to the mill, as did the one from Stocksbridge, so that by the time of their arrival, much damage had been done.

The Dixon's realized that the mill at Oughtibridge was not ideally located, as wood pulp was costly to tranship. An agreement with The Manchester, Sheffield & Lincolnshire Railway resulted in them building the railway siding from Oughtibridge station to the works. To ensure that they had control over their raw materials they eventually owned their own pulp mill in Finland and formed their own shipping company to bring the pulp to Grimsby. In 1905 they built the West Marsh mill, a few miles from the docks at Immingham. At the opening of the mill by Lord Northcliffe who, as Alfred Harmsworth, had been a friend of Mr. Joseph Dixon for many years, it was described as "the perfect mill". What attracted the Dixon's to Grimsby was that, apart from being on the coast, the town of 90,000 people had a direct railway line to London which was used mainly for the transportation of fish to the Capital and, as Dixon's had obtained major contracts for the supply of newsprint for the Daily Mirror and other London papers, it would provide a speedy and convenient means of delivery.

The Great War of 1914-1918 saw members of the Dixon family serving in the forces along with many of their employees. Immediately after the war was a boom period until the depression of 1925 and 1926 when the General Strike took place. Even so both mills were kept running, due to the loyalty of the workers, who recognised that Dixon's paid high wages and were good employers and that working conditions were better than most.

Joseph Dixon had always recognised that a settled work force was essential for a prosperous company and this was reflected in the way Dixon's became local benefactors supporting local organisations and functions for many years. In the 19th and early 20th Century he relied on the immediate area to provide his labour force and did much to ensure that conditions were improved wherever possible. In 1875 he had already bought seven houses, one shop and three acres of land at Wharncliffe Side from Marmaduke Pickles for £1085, to provide housing for some of his workers. In 1887 he along with others financed the building of Wharncliffe Side school and also offered to pay 50% of the cost of a District Nurse for the two villages. Another of his generous gestures to the area took place on 23rd October 1911, when he, along with Joseph Turner, Joseph Ridley and Cuthbert Dixon, purchased land at Oughtibridge from The Duke of Norfolk for £500. To celebrate the Coronation of King George V and Queen Mary, they formed a trust to administer a public park which became known as Coronation Park. On 5th November 1924. the Trustees conveyed the land to Bradfield Parish Council who have administered and improved the Park until it is now the delightful place we know today.

Glen Howe Park at Wharncliffe Side was purchased by Joseph Dixon and John Mills for £1000, and in 1917 the park was presented to Wortley Rural District Council. With the demise of that council, responsibility has passed to Sheffield City Council. Approximately 25 acres of magnificent woodland valley was set aside for public recreation and when the New Mill Pack Horse Bridge, which was erected by Benjamin Milnes in 1734 and which got its name from the corn mill situated in the Ewden valley, was threatened with destruction by the water works extensions, Joseph it should be re-erected in the park. Sadly, he was not to see this done as he died on 8th December 1926, aged 77 years. Three years after his death, his children arranged for the bridge to be moved, stone by stone, and is now in situ in the park, high up on the hill side over the Tinker Brook as it flows down the valley.

The passing of Joseph Dixon was mourned by many in all walks of life, from lowly villagers, to representatives from every phase of civic and industrial life. One review in the Worlds Paper Trade journal commented "the paper making industry of this country is robbed of a great personality. Mr. Dixon held a unique place in the ranks of British paper makers and he leaves an indelible impression upon the records of the industry." A fitting epitaph to a truly remarkable man.

The funeral service was held at Bradfield Parish Church on 11th December 1926 and workers were given the day off from work. As a mark of respect to this kind and generous man, the workers lined the road outside the factory as the cortege passed on its way to Bradfield. In 1930 a beautiful stained glass window was unveiled in Bradfield Church by the Bishop of Sheffield, Dr. Burrows, which was donated by his children in memory of Mr. Joseph Dixon and his wife, Mary.

Mr. Cuthbert Dixon took over control of the mill at Oughtibridge and continued to live at Spring Grove for a time. It was in 1937 that the district lost yet another of its close ties with the Dixons, with the death in her 90th year of Mr. Joseph Dixon's sister, Sarah Denison Dixon, who lived at "Woodside", adjoining Coronation Park in Oughtibridge. Three years earlier she had lost her lifelong friend, Mary Firth, who had been her nurse for 52 years. Miss Sarah was buried in Oughtibridge churchyard and the beautifully carved reredos in Oughtibridge Church was erected in her memory. Shortly before the outbreak of war Mr. Cuthbert Dixon took up duties in London, where, during the war years 1942-1945 he occupied an important position in the papermaking industry, guiding it through three of its most difficult years with much skill.

With the outbreak of war in 1939, Dixons found themselves in the front line as their Head Office was located in Fleet Street in London and was at great risk from the German bombing. Many of the company records were moved away from the Capital for safety, and the staff were evacuated to Oughtibridge where they were housed with families in the village. The Office Manager, Mr. Taylor, a refined and gentlemanly man lived with us for many months.

In 1935 the Spring Grove mill had changed from manufacturing newsprint to toilet tissues and production of tissue paper was also introduced. The following year saw an event which characterised the manner in which Dixon's treated their employees. In order to celebrate the forthcoming marriage of Mr. Bernard Dixon and also the coming of age of Mr. Peter Dixon, the company granted a general holiday to all its employees and arranged for them to be taken on an outing to London on 22nd June. This was organised in a most military manner with senior staff each being in charge of a group of employees who were instructed as to which carriage of the train they were to occupy and the precise times and details of all the days happenings. Different coloured badges were issued to identify workers from Oughtibridge, Grimsby and London. Special trains from Oughtibridge station and Grimsby were hired to transport everyone, the train from Oughtibridge leaving at 10-15 a.m. Lunch was taken on the train which arrived at Kings Cross at 2-23 p.m. Twenty-four coaches had been hired to take everyone on a tour of the Capital, and the souvenir programme detailed what buildings and places of note were on route. This was followed by a trip to Hampton Court where tea was provided. In the evening, after a meal in the Coventry Street Corner House, the entire party were entertained at the London Palladium before returning to Kings Cross for the return journey, arriving at Oughtibridge at 3-56 a.m. A similar outing was organised in 1953, when over 1000 employees of the company descended upon London to commemorate the Coronation and the 70th birthday of Lt-Col Oscar Dixon, T.D. All this may seem very ordinary by today's standard, but so many years ago, the majority of people had never been to the Capital and these were indeed days to remember. For many years, with transport almost non existent, the Dixon's relied on local people for their workforce and many families had a long connection with the mill. The writer's own family had over two hundred and fifty years service, with four members working for over fifty years. It was rare indeed for a worker to be dismissed and it was not unusual for an employee to continue working until he was well beyond the present retirement age. Such was the loyalty of Dixons to their staff and the workers to the company.

In the 1920's and 1930's with works canteens still some years into the future, many employees would take sandwiches to eat at Lunch time, whilst others who lived nearby would rush home for a quick meal. A lucky few would have a hot meal brought to the mill, usually by one of the younger members of the family who would be in serious trouble if the meal did not arrive at the mill in time for it to be placed on the Time Office table before the one o'clock hooter sounded. My own memories are of dashing home from school after the schoolmaster's daily announcement at five minutes to twelve that, "Dinner takers may leave now", running down Brook Lane, crossing the Coumes stream, up the steep bank and over the open field to come out half way up Jossey Lane, to arrive at home, red faced and breathless. After a quick meal, the hot dinner that Mother had carefully covered in warm cloths and packed in the purpose built, wickerwork basket, had to be carried up Crag View, down the "Rocks", a steep cliff face with a difficult rock strewn footpath to negotiate, all the while endeavouring not to spill the gravy and praying that the dreaded hooter would not sound.

Although times were often difficult in the 1930's, Dixons still recognised the need to keep up the morale of their employees. They had purchased a sports ground in Littlefield Lane at Grimsby and it became an annual event for a trip to be organised between the two mills, when sports activities and entertainment were provided.

In recent years various company reconstruction, amalgamations and changes have resulted in the mill at Oughtibridge having several changes to its name. With the introduction of the manufacture of facial and toilet tissues in 1963 it became British Tissues Ltd. and was known nationally for its brand name "Dixcel". This coincided with the last association of the Dixon's with the area, when Mr. Philip Dixon, who had continued to live at Spring Grove from 1946, moved to London. In later years changes in the ownership of the company resulted in it becoming known as Jamont's and more recently as Fort James, (U.K.) Ltd.

OTHER INDUSTRY

With so many of our major industries consigned to history, the list would not be complete without mention of the smaller concerns which once were an important part of village life. Several of these existed along Forge Lane but others have also passed into history. Along Wheel Lane, as the name implies, the water wheel, powered by water from Coumes brook, serviced the small Wagtail Wheel corn mill which stood near to where a house now stands. Another corn mill, now demolished and known for many years as Jarvill's mill, stood alongside Church Street in Oughtibridge. The dam, which again took its water from Coumes brook, still remains to remind us of the industry there. In the 1950's, although a listed building, the mill had fallen into such a dilapidated state that it was considered dangerous and was eventually demolished and the site used as a transport depot.

Another well known enterprise in the 1920's and 1930's was the mineral water business run by 'Poppy' Lees, using water from Bank Well spring. From the premises alongside the Coumes brook and New Street, opposite the White Hart Inn, he bottled his mineral waters in glass stoppered Codd bottles which had the design of the Bank Well Spring well on them and are now collectors items. The gas pressure inside the bottle held the glass ball against a rubber seal in the neck of the bottle. Utopia indeed, to be given a coin to buy one of his 'Penny Pops` on a hot Summers day.

Along at Wharncliffe Side was yet another corn mill at Spring Grove, whilst at Bedford House farm along Forge Lane, another enterprise flourished for a short time. With the introduction by the Government of a free one third pint of milk to schoolchildren, Arthur Hayward was amongst the first to contract to supply the several thousand bottles required every week-day. The installation of one of the latest bottling machines presented no problem with the filling of the bottles, but the washing and scouring by hand of every bottle, by family and friends, eventually proved too difficult and the enterprise ceased.

Lastly, a final mention of the occupation which, in the last century provided employment for many men in the district. Early Census returns show the large number who were employed as File Cutters, some in their own premises but many in the little workshops scattered throughout the area.

BUILDINGS, PLACES AND PEOPLE

HAYWARD'S BUTCHERS SHOP. Situated in the centre of Oughtibridge, it is perhaps a good place to start our look at some of the buildings and places in the district and of the people who lived there. It stood at the corner of Church Street and New Street, now Langsett Road North, and had large glass windows facing on to both streets. Above the windows was a wooden canopy, colloquially known as 'Hayward's Shed' under which many of the local characters would stand and gossip. A regular visitor there was a gentleman who I had cause to remember for two reasons. The first was that he had the same surname as myself, a fact that I did not discover until some time later, the other for a more painful reason. To a six year old, everyone over forty seems old, and I suppose he must have been about sixty years of age. Known locally as 'Dickie Pink', he was a man of medium height who's most prominent feature was a large stomach, no doubt resulting from his frequent visits to one or other of the five Public Houses within one hundred yards from Hayward's. On the way home from school one day in the 1920's, I was persuaded to ask him for the time, and, approaching him very politely, as one did in those days, I asked, "Please, Mr. Pink, could you tell me the time?", whereupon he gave me a cuff around the ears and told me not to be so bloody cheeky. Another story associated with him was that on his visits to the 'Shed', he would periodically release a most enormous belch which, repute has it, could be heard at the Silica Top Yard.

The entrance to the shop had three semi-circular stone steps leading into a room in which George Henry Hayward sold his meat. Above the shop was a large room known as The Assembly Rooms, in which dances were held from time to time at week-ends and which are no doubt responsible for this account being written. My mother and her sisters walked from Cliffe House farm at Dungworth to the dances and it was there that she met my father, who she later married, whilst her sister met Charles Hayward, the brother to George Henry. They later farmed at Bedford House Farm, along Forge Lane.

Adjoining the shop, in Church Street, was another building in which the animals were killed. It had large doors similar to many seen on local farms, which, when closed, left a tiny crack through which children, on the way to school, would try and get a glimpse of the grizzly business within. George Henry kept his cattle awaiting slaughter along Wheel Lane, in fields at Coldwell. He fetched the animal to be killed early on a Monday morning and he had learned from experience, that it was no good taking the one animal, as it could smell death on him and would be up every gennel and entry in Church Street. Humane killers had not been introduced in those days and the poor beast was suspended in chains before being bled to death.

Haywards Shop with "SHED"

Oughtibridge - Main Road. c 1910.

Cock Inn - Oughtibridge c 1900.

White Hart - Oughtibridge.

Blue Ball Inn - Worrall

Shoulder of Mutton - Worrall

Stanley Arms before demolition at Junction of Church Street and Top Road Oughtibridge.

Filesmiths Arms. Oughtibridge. Now a shop.

Morgans Shop - Church Street c 1910

Post Office Staff - Oughtibridge c 1910

THE WHITE HART. Located at the junction of Langsett Road North and Orchard Street, or Pea Lane as it was known in earlier times, the Inn is built over the Coumes Brook as it rushes down to join the Don. In the last century it had associations with the sport of Hound Trailing whilst as long ago as 1825 the Publican was Ann Bramall. Older people will remember it for the parrot, owned by the landlord who, I believe, in the 1920's was a Mr. Tricket, and who, during the summer months, would place the bird on the wall of what is now the entrance porch to the living quarters. Children returning from school would encourage the bird to talk, in the hope that it would repeat some of the choice language it had been taught by the customers.

In years past, as in the last war, families who lived in the country would resort to keeping a pig in order to provide meat and, occasionally, one would be killed at the White Hart. Food for the pig was often provided by several families who would save potato peelings and other scraps, on the understanding that they would receive an agreed share of the unfortunate animal. Several feet below what is now the car park, is a flagged area alongside the brook, where, in 1928, four men were having difficulty in holding a pig on the killing barrow whilst several children watched the proceedings through the railings above. Glancing up, one of the men called out, "Can one of you give a hand?", whereupon my brother, a sturdy lad of thirteen who spent much of his time at Bedford House Farm, immediately volunteered and was given the job of holding on to the pigs tail for all he was worth.

THE COCK INN. Situated in the middle of what was the oldest part of Oughtibridge, at the junction of Orchard Street and Bridge Hill, or Cock Hill as it was previously called, it was the centre for most of the village activities during the nineteenth century. Many of the old cottages, Little Mester's workshops and out-buildings that existed in close proximity to the Inn, have since been demolished. An uncle of mine who suffered from the effects of gas poisoning in the 1914/1918 war lived in one of them. The Smithy has been incorporated as part of the Inn and what was once the Bowling Green is now the car park. Before the Chapels were built, religious gatherings took place in a room there and political meetings were held in the forecourt at election time. Friday nights appear to have been a busy time with visiting traders bringing their wares. People could buy from the Pot stall or enjoy the entertainment provided by the man with his performing bear. One story concerning the latter, tells how one of the locals, having imbibed a little too freely with the local brew, decided to sleep it off and found a corner in a small out-house only to find next morning when he awoke that he had shared the room with the performing bear.

It would appear that the Brewery have made a mistake, as the sign above the entrance depicts a Cockerel, when, logic has it, that it should be a horse. Situated as it is, at the lowest point in the village, with steep hills up Church Street, Cockshutts Lane and Station Lane, the Cock horse of Nursery Rhyme fame was stabled there and whenever a horse drawn cart or dray had to negotiate one of the hills, an extra horse had to be attached to give a pull up the hill. I remember seeing the heavy steel chains being coupled to the cart shafts in order to get up Cockshutts Lane.

THE STATION INN. Dated back to the last century when the railway was a great asset to the village, the Inn no longer exists and the building is in use as a private dwelling. It is chiefly remembered for the dancing that took place there on a wooden platform at the rear of the Inn, to the accompaniment of the village band. This was perhaps a command performance, as the Landlord, in 1890, was George Fairest, who was one of the founder members of the Band. When the station was opened on 22 December 1845, the Station Master was George Smith.

THE PHEASANT INN holds special memories for me as, in 1933, along with several others, we had to pass it twice a day on the way to the station, in order to catch the train to take us to school at Woodhouse. In those days this area was part of the West Riding and the only Grammar Schools available to children in the Bradfield Parish were at Penistone and Woodhouse. Coming home at night the boys invariably made a practice of walking on the raised frontage of the Inn and climbing over the spiked railings, in order to walk on the top of the wall which ran alongside the allotments that were there in those days. The Landlord didn't take too kindly to this and his warnings had gone unheeded until, on one occasion, his dog came charging round the corner of the Inn as the last of the boys was about to climb the spiked fence. The boy, in his haste to escape the attention of the dog, failed to ensure that he cleared the fence properly, with the result that the spikes slid smoothly inside his jacket, fixing him firmly to the railings whilst the dog barked furiously a few inches from his head.

THE TRAVELLERS REST was certainly in business over a hundred years ago but just how old it is, is not known.

THE HARE AND HOUNDS. The building dates back to the last century with the 1861 Census listing Charles Greaves as the Landlord.

THE MIDDLEWOOD TAVERN. Still in business at the corner of Hangman and which I believe in earlier times was known as The Corporation Arms.

THE STANLEY ARMS, stood at the corner of Church Street and Top Road, facing The Filesmiths Arms, on what is now the Westnall House site. What was the origin of the name? Something to do with Livingstone I presume, or maybe members of the Stanley family can claim that the name was theirs as the Publican in 1833 was Martin Stanley.

THE FILESMITHS ARMS. No longer a Public House. Situated on Langsett Road, facing Westnall House, it is still in use as a shop. In 1849 the Landlord was John Holdsworth whilst Henry Ibbotson appears to have been in charge from 1862 to 1876 and again some ten years later.

THE TRAVELLERS INN, WHARNCLIFFE SIDE. The Lingard family were well known in the district in the nineteenth century and the Lingard's were listed as Publicans from 1841 to the 1870's. Robert Lingard as well as being a publican is recorded as a Cutler and Spindle Maker whilst his son Robert was also the Landlord at the Travellers Inn in 1871 and was also a Spindle Maker and Spring Knife manufacturer. My own family were closely associated with the Lingards as my Great Grandfather's brother George, married Robert's sister, Sophia Lingard and was in business as Sanderson and Lingard, Spindle Manufacturers with Robert.

THE SHOULDER OF MUTTON, WORRALL. Inside, it bears little resemblance to the old village Inn of years ago. Now extended and modernised, only the older residents remember it as it was, with its Snug and local carols at Christmas. One reminder from the past, is the old blacksmiths anvil block mounted near to the dining room, which was once a cottage. Just how old the Inn is, is hard to establish, but what is known is that the well known local Charlesworth family were Landlords there early in the nineteenth century, with William in charge in 1825 and Joseph in 1841. In earlier years, the ground at the rear was used as the site for a Fair, when stalls were illuminated by paraffin lamps or candles. Visiting tradesmen would come with their wares, whilst entertainment would be provided by the Tingalary man and his organ and the man with his performing bear. Life was often difficult, with many houses relying on outside troughs for water, whilst, in hard winters, those houses with water laid on to the kitchen sink, had to fetch supplies from what were known as 'Tanks'. These were frequently frozen, and water had to be drawn from the village troughs or, on extreme occasions, from the well, where the cattle were also taken. With no electricity, gas, buses or telephone, the villagers were isolated and had to rely on begging a lift on the horse drawn milk float or other horse drawn transport, to the trams at the bottom of Wadsley Lane.

The area around the Inn has changed a great deal in recent years. Houses now stand where open fields stretched down to the rear of the Chapel. Buildings at the corner of Top Road and Kirk Edge Road near to the cross roads were for many years part of Worrall Hall farm across the road which was farmed by Mr Vic Codd. The buildings were demolished to allow the Lund estate to be built. Jack Shepherd was busy farming at Grange Farm across the road alongside Kirk Edge Road on which the estate has been built. Near to the farm was a cottage and "Little Mester's" workshop. Some fifty yards away, near to Worrall Road, stood a wooden hut on a small piece of land alongside the stream which rushed down the hillside This was used for several years by Mr and Mrs Taylor who lived in the Owlerton district, as a base for their newspaper delivery business. They deserve a mention in any record of the village as with age and sickness they still continued to deliver papers until it was finally too much. Many people in the area will remember their son, Ivan, who in spite of his disabilities, for many years was an ardent follower of the local cricket and football teams and who, although residing in a care home at the opposite side of town, regularly visited this area until his death. A modern bungalow now stands astride the stream before it tumbles into the village troughs. One of the few photographs taken of the old cottages that existed on Towngate Road at the junction with Top Road, shows Mrs. Alliban standing in the doorway of the flat topped cottage which served as the village Post Office.

THE BLUE BALL INN, WORRALL. Originally, it had a row of cottages attached, the end one of which was a small shop in which Old Mary Grayson sold home made Pikelets and Oatcakes. Old residents recall how they watched through the window as the Oatcakes bubbled up on the backstone. The Landlord at the end of the last century was John Grayson. Whether they were related is not known. Earlier, around 1850 the Landlord was a Mr Turner better known locally as a quarry owner. On the other side of the Inn was a wooden structure, part of which was a coal place in which the hounds of the local hunt from Ecclesfield were put whilst the huntsmen imbibed in a drink or two before starting the chase.

The Monday following the Chapel sermons was known as Worrall Feast, when a rather strange ceremony took place. Fred Gelder, along with other men, would march around the village in front of the band carrying long poles, before arriving back at The Blue Ball. Where the Feast took place is a matter for conjecture but it is known that local residents paid into a 'Club', presumably to pay for the meal. The Blue Ball remains one of the local Inns which encourages the tradition of singing the local carols at Christmas time. Beginning on the Sunday lunchtime following Remembrance Day, the singing attracts visitors from a wide area and over the years has received the attention of Television and Radio companies.

THE CHURCHES

Before the arrival of the nineteenth century there were no established religious centres in our area and anyone wishing to attend a service would be faced with a long journey to either Bradfield or Ecclesfield. Religious meetings were often held in rooms in private houses or in a room at a local Inn or at a street corner.

In Oughtibridge, in the years up to the second world war the Churches were a mainstay of village life with Youth Groups, Sunday School and other organisations sponsored by the churches flourishing for many years. In the last century, both the Parish Church and the Zion had their cricket clubs whilst Whitsuntide was a major event in the village. Even so, discord prevailed and the Chapels maintained their independence from the established Church by having their Witness and Sing on Whit Monday morning whilst the Church paraded in the afternoon. As a boy, I remember feeling aggrieved that the Chapels had the use of Coronation Park for their games whilst the Church had to make do with the field below the Cemetery. Today, with all the talk of Global Warming it seems a little strange, as often in the 1930's, the Whitsuntide walks were held in wonderfully warm weather. On one occasion I remember the tar melting at the bottom of Church Street, causing a problem for many in their best Whitsuntide outfits.

BRIGHTHOLMLEE METHODIST CHAPEL. The oldest of our religious buildings, dating back to 1807. Reputedly the oldest in Sheffield in which services are still held, it has associations with John Wesley.

THE ZION UNITED REFORM CHURCH. The first of the chapels to be built in Oughtibridge. With the upsurge of interest in the Methodist movement across the region, a group of devout men began holding open air meetings near to a workshop known as "The Tip and Shuttle" shop at the bottom of Orchard Street. Other meetings took place in a room in or near the Cock Inn until the members built the Zion chapel. The foundation stone was laid on the 11th March 1833 by Mr George Grayson and the Chapel was opened for Services on 18 July 1833, only four months later. The moral standards were very high in those days, as could be shown by the decision that no further communion with Mary Denton would be allowed until she confessed her sin and repented for marrying an unbeliever. In 1879, land adjoining the Chapel alongside the main road was purchased for use as a Sunday School, but it was some ten years before it came in to use. Later, in the early part of the Century, it was used as an auxiliary classroom for the village school during a period when the school population was rising rapidly.

THE METHODIST CHAPEL. Now demolished, it stood some yards up Church Street on what is now the Westnall House site. It was a typical two storey building, similar to many others built during the same period, with the chapel above and a room and vestry below. It has personal memories for me as I remember, in the 1920's, my father coming home from work on a Friday evening and, after a meal, changing into his best suit to go to the chapel for the regular weekly meeting of The Manchester Unity of Oddfellows which were held in the Vestry there. This was in the days before Beveridge introduced his plan for the Health Service and families relied on Sick Clubs to help them through a period when the family income ceased because of illness. People attended regularly to make their meagre contributions into the club or to sign on the 'Plonk' and draw the pittance, which was often just enough to keep a roof over the family. Most of the families in the village paid rent and no matter what else went short, the rent had to be paid, as the indignity and fear of being taken over the hill to Grenoside and the Workhouse, was dreaded by many. There were penalties attached to being on the club as a strict curfew was enforced and anyone reported as being out after eight o'clock was likely to be taken off benefit. For many years we had a large gilt framed, elaborately decorated scroll which had been presented to my father by the Oddfellows, in recognition of his time as President and sadly, it has been lost.

THE WESLEYAN REFORM CHAPEL. The middle of the nineteenth century appears to have been an unsettled time for the Methodist movement with members feeling so dissatisfied that they formed separate groups, and, after holding services in an upper room, eventually built their own place of worship. As a result the Wesleyan Reform Chapel was built in 1854.

THE PARISH CHURCH. With the rapid expansion of the population due to the Industrial Revolution, there was a growing demand for a place of worship for the members of the Church of England. In 1834 Wadsley Church was built and became responsible for the three 'bridge' areas of Wadsley Bridge, Malin Bridge and Oughtibridge. However, people in Oughtibridge were still faced with some distance to travel in order to attend a service and eventually were granted permission to have a Church of their own. On the 22nd June, 1842, the foundation stone of the Church at Oughtibridge was laid, but it did not become an independent cure until 19th June 1868. Although Oughtibridge is now a separate Parish, Wadsley still maintains a connection, in that the Vicar of Wadsley has duties regarding the appointment of a new vicar at Oughtibridge. Over the years the church has changed somewhat. Originally the two towers had minarets but one was damaged in a storm and the other was removed for safety. Inside, the stark interior of a century ago has been changed to the well appointed church of today. I remember, as a choirboy in 1930, the argueing that took place as to who's turn it was to pump the organ and woe to the one who fell asleep during the service and allowed it to run out of wind.

Of the Vicars who have officiated during the last one hundred and fifty years, the most controversial must surely have been the Rev. Wm. Rowthorne who was appointed Vicar in 1882. He campaigned vigorously against drinking and gambling, which was non too popular with many of the hard working, but poor, populace and things became so difficult in 1890 that a public meeting was organised at which he was urged to resign. However, he stayed on with a dwindling congregation and died in 1914. The history of the Church is well documented in the booklet by Jack Ambler.

WORRALL INDEPENDENT CHAPEL. Built in 1826 from local stone, in years past the schoolroom below was used as part of Worrall school. For many years it was a mainstay of village life with an active Church membership and Sunday School. The musical life of the Chapel was climaxed by the annual Sunday School Anniversary Sermons held every year on the second Sunday in July. Like many other chapel sermons in the area, it was held outdoors whenever possible with the children and church members seated on a substantial wooden platform erected against the chapel wall or convenient farmer's building. People from a wide area would visit Worrall to hear and join in the wonderful music which could include such masterpieces as 'Hallelujah Chorus' and 'The Heavens are telling'. All this was arranged to fit into the strict time-table with other chapels as many volunteer singers and musicians would do the rounds and support the various Sermons held over several weeks of the year. It was often a time of family re-union as distant relatives would make a point of visiting to see other members of the family. I can vouch for this as I remember, as a small boy of five, walking from Oughtibridge to Storr's for the Anniversary Sermons and afterwards meeting members of my mothers family before, late at night, trudging up Long Lane to Worrall as a thunder storm approached and seeing a fireball plummet to earth in the direction of Bradfield.

Brightholmlee Methodist Chapel

*Worrall Independent Chapel
From Hagg Stones Road. Worrall*

SCHOOLS

OUGHTIBRIDGE NATIONAL SCHOOL. The foundation stone was laid by the Earl of Wharncliffe in 1860 and the school came under the control of the Ecclesiastical District of Ecclesfield. The rapid expansion of the local population had resulted in more children attending the wooden Church School building situated in the corner of what is now the Churchyard. With some 200 children being taught in overcrowded conditions and classrooms having to be held in the Church, something had to be done and the Rev. W. Knight organised fund raising events in order to raise £600, being half the cost of £1200 needed. Early school records recount the animosity that existed between the Vicar and the Headmaster which, on more than one occasion, resulted in fisticuffs.

In those early years, conditions must have been very hard, with heat provided by a solid fuel cast iron stove in one corner of the room, so that in the middle of Winter, the pupils nearest the stove were too warm, whilst those some feet away were likely to be shivering from the cold. A visit to the toilet was an ordeal to be avoided if at all possible, as it entailed a dash across the school yard to the earth type middens where an icy blast of wind entering through the gaps at the top and bottom of the door, made it a bone chilling experience. Whether these harsh conditions were responsible for the death of one of the first teachers, Mr. James Andrews, who died at the early age of 25, on 23rd October, 1863, only two years after the school was opened and who is buried in the Churchyard, will never be known.

One teacher of the 1920's who is still remembered by local people, was Mr. J.P.Barrett. He was a strict disciplinarian and few pupils were brave enough to pass him or his wife on the street, without giving a smart salute. Any boy who failed to show respect could expect to be in trouble at school on the following day. His wife was also a teacher of classes two and three in the Zion Schoolroom, on Top Road. She was perhaps the only teacher to adopt the Four R's; Reading, 'Riting, 'Rithmatic and the fourth, Ringworms. Every week started with an inspection of the head to discover if any girl or boy had the complaint, which was all too common at that time and was no respector of persons.

Daily routine began with an inspection of hands and neck in search of the dreaded 'Tidemark'. With many very poor families in the district for whom soap was almost a luxury, it was quite common for some of the children to be sent down into the cellar, in the charge of a Monitor, to scrub up and remove the tell-tale sign. Access to the cellar was by means of a trapdoor in the centre of the room, which, when opened, revealed several stone steps leading down to a large room in which was a long stone sink, some four inches deep and eight feet long, taking up much of one wall.

Mrs. Barrett had two methods of maintaining discipline. She invariably carried a three inch long school issue whistle in her hand as she moved around the classroom examining the work on slate or exercise book of each of the pupils. Unsatisfactory work resulted in a tapping on the head with it as she issued a stern rebuke. Her other method of punishment was a rap across the knuckles with a twelve inch rule which left fingers tingling for the rest of the day. Although strict, Mrs. Barrett had her good points. It was not unknown for her to keep one or two backward children in her class for several years, and on one occasion this caused some merriment. A visiting School Inspector noticed that one boy, who shall be nameless, was busy rolling his thumbs around each other and was asked; "Boy, can't you do anything else but that?" Back came the reply "Yes, Sir. I can do that" as he rapidly rolled his thumbs in the opposite direction.

After the departure of the Barretts, the new Headmaster was Mr. Appleyard. Although less strict than Mr. Barrett, he still believed in the use of the cane and on one occasion this resulted in a boy's spirit being broken. The boy, who regularly received one or two strokes without showing any signs of discomfort, was about to be punished for something that he had not done, and on principle, refused to be caned. "Hold out your hand", came the command. "A'm not havin t'cane." "Hold out your hand." "Th'art not goin to gi'me cane." With no more to do, he dashed out of the classroom and ran home, to be followed shortly afterwards by four senior boys, detailed by the Headmaster to fetch him back to school. They arrived at the boy's home just in time to meet the runaway as he was being propelled back to school by his father, who had him in a grip by the scruff of his neck. Arriving in the school porch, what happened next could only be seen by a few, but with classrooms on three sides, most of the pupils could hear as the Headmaster was addressed by the boy's father, "Ar Ellis tells me he's run away from scoil. Ge'im a thrashin. A'm not avin 'im run away from scoil."

After a few seconds, the listening pupils heard the swish, swish, of the cane as the Headmaster delivered six of the best, whereupon the father was heard to say, "As tha finished? Here, ge'us it. A'm not avin' im run away from scoil", as he proceeded to thrash the boy. He never had the cane again.

An Assistant Master at that time, had the rather sinister name of Bill Sykes and he was a frequent user of the cane. On one occasion this gave rise to a rather humorous but painful incident. Mr. Sykes, on looking up from his desk, saw one boy on the rear row of desks in conversation with another. "Mallinson. Come here" he said as he crooked his finger. The only response was a shake of the head. "Mallinson, don't you know that when I do this, I want you to come here?" said the Teacher as he again repeated his finger movement. "Sir, don't you know that when I do this, I'm not bloody well coming", came the reply, with another shake of the head. What followed was a two minutes exercise in stalking, as the Master endeavoured to catch Mallinson, who successfully managed to keep two desks between them as they moved around the room. Eventually, when caught and put over the front desk for punishment, he was still not willing to accept punishment and kicked back with his feet on which was a sturdy pair of boots. He connected with the wrist of the teacher and shattered his nice new wrist watch, which were a rarity in those days.

One of the subjects taught in those early years was woodwork, which entailed pupils travelling to the school at Normandale. Children were provided with a halfpenny bus token for the journey from Worrall to Wadsley, but the rest of the way had to be on foot. It was not unknown for a pupil, after walking from Worrall at lunchtime, to try to sneak in to school in order to cut part way through the teacher's cane with a razor blade so that the first punishment meted out in the afternoon would cause a great deal of merriment as the cane broke in two.

WORRALL NATIONAL SCHOOL. Dating back to 1848, some twelve years before the National school at Oughtibridge, the land for the school was transferred to the Archdeacon of York by Thomas Hounsfield as the site for a school for the poor of the Parish of Ecclesfield and for a school house for the Headmaster or Mistress. The Committee of Management, consisted of the Minister of the Ecclesiastical District and included well known local benefactors, John Bedford of Wadsley, John Kenyon Skelton and Joseph Dixon Skelton of Middlewood and Samuel Gardner of Sheffield. The school was to be open at all reasonable times to the Inspectors, who's duties were to ensure that pupils were to be educated in the principals of the Established Church. Originally known as Worrall Church School it was some thirty years later that it became Worrall National School. For many years the schoolroom across the road in the Chapel was used as an extra classroom and later a pre-fabricated classroom was added.

The log-book of the school is still in existence at Sheffield Archive Office, Shoreham Street and reveals a glimpse of what conditions were like over a hundred years ago. Absenteeism was a major problem with often only half the pupils present due to sickness and other causes. Illness could be anything from typhoid, whooping cough, smallpox, scarletina, measles and the common cold, whilst other reasons for absence ranged from haymaking, bilberrying, potato picking, to the shortage of money to pay the school fees of a few pence per week in 1881.

In 1884 all boys over ten years of age had to attend Oughtibridge National School and in July 1964 the school was closed and the children transferred to the school at Oughtibridge. The building remained empty for several years until the inside was affected by dry rot which ruined the parquet block flooring. The building was eventually sold and is now a private dwelling. The Honours Board, listing the pupils from the school who passed the "County Minor" and went to Penistone Grammar School in the days of the old West Riding County Council is still in the Independent Chapel.

THE OLD SCHOOL HOUSE. Situated along Wheel Lane, a short distance below Onesacre, the building is now a private residence. In the nineteen sixties it narrowly missed demolition when it was declared unfit for habitation, but fortunately it has been renovated and is now a jewel in our countryside as it stands on the hillside overlooking the Coumes brook. Part of the property dates back to the twelfth century and for much of that time was a school. There was certainly a school there in the seventeenth century. I remember my Grandfather recounting how, in the last century, he walked from Sykehouse Farm at Dungworth to be educated there, at a cost of two pence a week.

In 1087 it was recorded in the Domesday survey that there was a one up - one down building on the site which was described as Ansacre, a manor held by the Saxon, Godric. In 1797, Thomas Steade bequeathed the sum of £50 and other persons including Sarah Greaves of Worrall donated £100 to a trust which was formed "to encourage a fit person or persons to instruct at or near Onesacre, as many poor children, not less than twelve, born or residing within the districts of Onesacre, Oughtibridge or Worrall, as the trustees should think fit." Income for the Trust came mainly from the purchase of one third of the rents from a farm at Wigtwizzle owned by Robert Hawke, the other two thirds going to Brigg's Charity at Sproatley, in the East Riding. The school was closed in 1886 due to "the inadequacy of requirements of Education Act" and in the following year the school at Wharncliffe Side was opened. The school bell on the corner of the building was replaced by a previous owner.

WHARNCLIFFE SIDE SCHOOL. Dating back to 1886, the school was built by public subscription. The Dixon family, who at that time must have been relative newcomers to the area, donated the land and other worthies donated various sums of money, from 1/- by John Bramall, to £25 by John Hudson. Other money came from a Gala held in Glen Howe, whilst Chas Hodgkinson gave one dozen Duplex oil lamps, valued at two Guineas, and the Ploughing Society £2. The total cost of the school was expected to be between £600 and £700. The opening of the school at Wharncliffe Side appears to have been a deciding factor in the closure of Onesacre School.

SHOPS

THE CO-OPERATIVE SOCIETY. For many years it was the biggest shop in the village, with its three departments, Grocery, Millinery and Butchery and a branch shop on Town Gate at Worrall, now a private dwelling. During the early years of the Century, it formed an important part of village life as most families had a Co-op number and relied on the 'Divi' to provide that little extra cash for new clothes at Whitsuntide or presents at Christmas. Elections to the Committee were serious affairs and well known personalities were pleased to serve, as it carried with it a certain degree of importance. There were many long serving employees. Mr. George Plant was the Manager for many years with Miss Ada Walters, Mr. George Hurst and Mr. Castle on the Staff. As a small boy, one errand I never minded doing, was having to fetch a bag of flour for Mother to bake bread on the Yorkshire Range. At the rear of the shop was a room in which two or three kinds of flour were stored in large open bins, and it was a thrill to be allowed to use the large flour scoop to fill a brown paper bag with the wonderfully soft flour and then be allowed to weigh it on the large weighing scales, under the watchful eye of Mr. Bert Barratt, who was for many years the Organist at the Church and later, the Choir Master.

Stocktaking, undertaken by members of the Committee, was a serious affair and the announcement of what the 'Divi' was to be, was greeted with a fair amount of interest. For several days after the announcement, the General Office above the Millinery Department was kept busy as members collected their cash or, for a few who were better off, had it recorded in their Share Book. In the 1930's the Co-op acquired a flat bed lorry which they garaged on a piece of land near to the Stanley Arms and which Mr. Gould drove for many years.

TOBY PRESTON'S. Situated at the top of Orchard Street, facing The White Hart, this small shop was the village Drug Store. The entrance was on the corner and had semi-circular stone steps to the entrance. To the children of the time, it seemed a bit like getting into Fort Knox as, upon opening the door, a large overhead bell clanged, whilst one step inside on to the mat well, caused a buzzer to sound. This was necessary as Mr. Preston was often busy developing and printing the films from the Box cameras and Brownies of the time. He did this in his dark room upstairs, which meant that a customer had to wait a little while for him to come to the shop. Children would often cause him annoyance, as first one child and then another would enter the shop after he had returned upstairs, each one requiring a half-pennyworth of sweets, which were invariably in a glass jar on the top shelf. Before it became a Drug Store, I believe it was a Drapery Shop run by a Mrs. Hutchinson.

MRS. EDWARDS. Facing the bottom of Cockshutts Lane, this little shop provided many hours of enjoyment for children as they looked longingly at the wonderful selection of sweets for sale. A halfpenny could buy a surprising variety of things. A yard of liquorice Telephone Wire, five small toffees each individually wrapped, Bulls Eyes, Gob-Stoppers that changed colour as they were sucked, bags of Kali to be sucked through a straw, sweet cigarettes in packets of five or ten, and many others. What really made one's day, was to be given the cigarette card out of a packet as a customer left the shop, and the joy if it completed the set. What great sets the cigarette cards made and how much enjoyment they provided as they were mounted in their albums. What wonderful series there were. Film Stars, Cricketers, Steam Locomotives, Animals, Flowers and a host of others. The beautiful sets of silk flags in the packets of Kensitas cigarettes are now collectors pieces. The children of the 20's and 30's often learned more from the cigarette cards than they did at school, whilst the accumulation of 'spares' was never a problem as they provided cards for the game of skims. This required a certain amount of skill, as the idea was to hit a card placed up against a wall by flicking or skimming another card from several feet away. Players took it in turns and the winner collected all the cards that were 'misses'. What a variety of cigarettes there were. Will's Woodbines, often referred to as coffin nails, Park Drive, Kensitas, in packets of 20 with a small packet of four cigarettes for the ladies stuck on the side, Player's Weights, Senior Service, Little Queens, Gold Flake, Black Cat, Three Darts, complete with three matches, Capstan, Robin, Churchman and many others.

FRANK HAYWARD'S. The shop was one of the old buildings bordering on to New Street, which later became Langsett Road North. Demolished some years ago, it faced the Cock Inn and was only a few yards from his brother's butchers shop. He sold cakes and other delicacies from the small shop which, as a young boy, always seemed to me to be poorly stocked and rather gloomy, but my memories are chiefly of having to fetch a half pennyworth of barm for Mother to bake bread. Nothing seemed so delicious as the nibbling at the yeast on the way home. Frank Hayward was a gentle man who enjoyed a gossip with his lady customers and, although he could hardly be called a sporting type, he did win some thousands of pounds on the Irish Sweep Stake. A small fortune in those days.

JARVILL'S SHOP. Half way up Church Street, Mrs. Jarvill sold sweets to children on the way to school from the window of the living room in the house adjoining the old Corn Mill. The house was later used as an office for a transport company.

THE OLD POST OFFICE. Situated along Langsett Road North in Oughtibridge near to the Zion Chapel, it is now a private dwelling. Around a century ago it was the Post Office and later a fish and chip shop known locally as Emma Cheethams.

OTHER SHOPS. England was for many years referred to as a nation of shop keepers and this was certainly true of Oughtibridge almost a hundred years ago. Before 1913, when the first bus service started, it was very much a self contained community with an abundance of shops supplying most of the families needs, from food, clothing, drinks and newspapers, to items of hardware, saddlery from the Saddler's shop next to the Filesmiths Arms, coffins from my Grandfather's joiners shop in the old Toll Bar cottage at the bottom of Cockshutts Lane and items from the Post Office. Travelling salesmen supplied other items much in use, as did the weekly pot stall at The Cock Inn. In the 1920's, Jackie Padget would give you a 'Basin cut' haircut in his premises on Glossop Row, 'Cobbler' Sanderson would repair your shoes. The Rag and Bone man would exchange Donkey Stone for use on the door-steps or window sills, or balloons or a gold fish, for a bundle of rags. How many children on hearing the familiar cry "Balloons for rags", would rush inside the house for a few rags, only to be told by the Rag and Bone man that there was not enough for a balloon. Black lead for polishing the fire place and paraffin could be obtained from Parkins hardware shop on Top Road. I remember the large drum just inside the entrance where one had to pump the handle to fill a paraffin can. They also sold gas mantles, which became more and more a necessity as houses were supplied with gas, leaving only isolated country homes with paraffin lamps. Across the road was the shop which I had to visit as one of my weekly errands. The early days of wireless meant all sets were battery operated and every Saturday morning I had the job of taking the two volt accumulator to be recharged by Jack Staniforth and bring back a charged one, after making sure it had our name on it. It must seem a little primitive in these days of electricity but I remember it was quite an expense when the 120 volt HT battery with its 9 Volt Grid Bias had to be bought. In earlier times the shop had been the Filesmiths Arms.

Among well known local families of the past, the 1891 Census included Eli Morton who had a Greengrocer's business on Zion Terrace. Emily Tricket had a Drapery business there and nearby, Sarah Hirst sold provisions from her shop. Abigail Fairest kept a News Agency and Jane Crookes kept the Post Office on Top Road. Sarah Hutchinson had a Milliners shop on New Street and William Morton had a Greengrocers shop there. John Hayward had the butchers shop. He must have been the father of George Henry Hayward who has already been mentioned. Charles Jarvill was busy at the Corn Mill up Church Street and to show how rural Oughtibridge was in those times, George Woodhouse was listed as a farmer and horse carter at Birch House. Tonk's shop stood at the corner of Glossop Row and Top Road and Jack Tonks in 1915 could be relied on to supply a variety of clothes for children including blue and white sailor suits from 1/11d. or Ready to Wear suits for men and boys from 15/6d.

OTHER BUILDINGS

THE TOLL BAR COTTAGES. Of the two Toll Bars that once existed in Oughtibridge, only one of the buildings has survived. Facing the entrance to Middlewood Hall, the renovated white walled cottage stood at the point where an access road led towards a ford over the river Don. The road ran alongside the river for some two hundred yards before reaching the ford, several feet wide, which is still in a remarkably good condition. It enabled the horse drawn carts and drays to save a great amount of time and effort when they were heading for the industries on Clay Wheel Lane and Wadsley Bridge. Another ford crossing existed facing the bottom of Stockarth Lane.

The second Turnpike stood at the bottom of Cockshutts Lane. The cottage was demolished when the narrow country lane was widened. It has personal memories for me as it was the workshop for my Grandfather's joinery business. In those days coffins were often less substantial affairs than in later years, with many poor families in the area. Upon the death of an individual, a coffin would be made quickly and carried to the house where the body was laid out and prepared for burial by one of the ladies of the district who were well known for carrying out this unpleasant task. An old photograph shows a pole carrying a solitary telephone wire to Peter Dixon and Son Ltd. paper mill at Spring Grove, the first telephone in the village known as Oughtibridge National No.1

THE READING ROOM. The fore-runner of Oughtibridge Comrades Club, it was situated in Orchard Street and in the 1920's members met there to enjoy a game of snooker or read the newspapers. The snooker table was upstairs and I remember the Caretaker was a Mr. Heath who kept guard on the door and soon moved any child who ventured too near. Eventually it was converted into two houses and Mr. Robert Sensicall lived there for many years.

HIGH LEA FARM, BRIGHTHOLMLEE. One of the few remaining houses built on the Cruck principle.

ONESACRE HALL. Records show that there were buildings at Onesacre in the eleventh century which were mentioned in the Domesday survey and that even earlier the lands at Onesacre formed part of the estate of Godric, the Saxon Lord. For many years the present buildings which date back to 1580, were allowed to fall into a state of disrepair but recent renovation has rescued them from their ruinous state. Before the renovations, visitors could find the remains of a Cock Pit in the roof area where no doubt the cruel sport of cock fighting was carried out. Two Cruck Barns have been converted into dwellings but a further one is in urgent need of repair.

In the 1920's, Tophill Farm or Low farm, as it was sometimes called, was farmed by Mr. Joe Wood who for many years delivered milk in Oughtibridge in his milk float. This was before the days of the milk bottle when people took a jug to the cart and the milk was dispensed straight from the milk churn with the long handled pint, half pint or gill measuring cans. One of his fields at the top of Cockshutts Lane, known as The Myers, although on a steep slope and very uneven, had one small area which was flat and was used by the children in Crag View as a football pitch. Mr. Wood had warned the children on more than one occasion about playing there, and on one cold, frosty November morning he arrived with his farmhand 'Curly', and two dogs, whilst an important game between the Roadenders and the Cragviewers was in progress. As was customary, the boys had removed coats and caps, which were used as goal posts, and were so intent on the game that they failed to see the farmer until it was too late. Departing in such haste that coats were left behind, they stood around shivering, and watching as the piles of coats were loaded on to the cart. A shouted message that they could have them back when they fetched them from Onesacre was greeted with dismay. Realising that they had no other option, they followed the cart, some yards behind, and upon arriving at the farm, were admitted one at a time into the kitchen where they were given a smack on the backside and let out of a rear door with a warning about not playing in the field again.

RURAL COTTAGE. This cottage at Onesacre has interesting connections with the Crusades in the twelfth century, when King Richard was away fighting the Saracens in the Holy Land. The 9th and 10th centuries saw pilgrims from all over Europe visiting The Holy Land and after travelling for many weeks over land and sea, large numbers arrived sick or injured, often dying from fatigue or ill treatment. French and other European Knights who had taken a vow of poverty and chastity, sought and obtained permission from the Caliph of Egypt to build a hospital in Jerusalem to treat the pilgrims. The hospital was finished in 1048 and dedicated to St. John the Baptist. The Knights later became known as The Knights Hospitaller Brothers of St. John of Jerusalem and wore a black robe with an eight pointed white cross on the breast. With the need to defend Jerusalem, other Knights formed a military arm which became known as The Knights Templars. As the wars of The Crusades continued, the Knights suffered defeats and were eventually driven out of Palestine in 1291. The Hospitallers settled in Cyprus until 1310 and then moved to Rhodes where they stayed for almost two hundred years. The grand Master of the Order persuaded Emperor Charles V of France to grant them the island of Malta, where they stayed until 1798 when Napoleon seized the island. Visitors to that island can still see the large rectangular stone buildings in Valetta that housed the Knights of the various countries. The 12th century saw many of the Knights returning home, where they became the owners of some one hundred and eight manors throughout the country including the manor of Waldershelf.

A Papal Bull dated 1141 refers to Bradfield and its four Byrlaws, Waldershelf, Westnall, Bradfield and Dungworth, where the Knights Hospitallers owned about twelve houses in this area. Their tenants, many of whom had no doubt provided sons to accompany the knights as servants, or retainers, were allowed to carve emblems on the corbels of the houses to denote that they were excused from paying taxes, tithes, tolls and fair fees. Rural Cottage was one such building with another at Ughill. On 7th May 1540, the Priory at Clerkenwell which was the main seat of the Knights, was dissolved and the vast estates and monastic buildings belonging to them were broken up over a period of several years.

Tony Nicholson in his notes in the Parish magazine mentioned how one small part of the ancient hamlet was known as Haslaigh and was mentioned in the Sheffield Manorial records in 1315. Around 1380 John Stead of Wentworth married Alice le Rous who was the sole heiress to the estate of Le Rous at Onesacre which had been held in her family for over a hundred years. Later, lands at Onesacre were held by the Stead family for over 400 years.

THE CARMELITE CONVENT. High up on the edge of the moors at Kirk Edge, the building has an interesting history. As far as I can ascertain, the original building there in the nineteenth century was said to be a farm which was later used as an Orphanage. The boys and girls housed there were obliged to earn money towards their keep by laundering for people in the area. At one time it was a common sight to see the boys pushing a large barrow around the district in which they collected the laundry and took it back to the Orphanage for the girls to wash and iron, ready to be returned the following week. This continued until an incident took place at Liverpool, which was to affect the Orphanage. Boys with a criminal background were housed in a ship moored in the Mersey and whether by design or intent, the ship caught fire and accommodation had to be found very quickly for the inmates. Some were housed in the Orphanage for a period. All this must have been before 1871 for around that time the premises were used as a Roman Catholic girls orphanage and industrial school where the girls were instructed in all manner of household duties until the premises were closed in 1885.

The buildings must have remained empty for a number of years for it was not until the early part of this century in 1911 that the buildings were used as a Convent. The sister to the Duke of Norfolk was keenly interested in the Carmelite movement and was actively seeking premises in Yorkshire for use as a convent. When the Duke offered her the Orphanage, it was accepted and a chapel was built and other buildings modified to their present use. The inauguration ceremony would appear to have been an event of some importance as the Sheffield Independent reported that approaching one thousand people walked to the isolated Convent on the moors above Sheffield, when twelve ladies took vows of silence and were incarcerated, as the Roman Catholic Bishops of Liverpool and Leeds officiated. Still in use today, Census returns inform us of the number of Nuns at the Convent but the passage of time has slowly seen changes as around the middle of the twentieth century, local residents and Roman Catholic Priests could regularly be seen walking to the Convent in order to attend the services.

HILL HOUSE FARM. Situated high on the hillside above Burnt Hill, it was the birthplace of the district's most notorious murderer. Francis Fearn was born there on 25th May 1760 and in 1778 was apprenticed to John Wilkinson, a filesmith on West Bar Green in Sheffield. It was in Sheffield that he met Nathan Andrews, a jeweller of High Street and persuaded him to visit a non-existent Watch Club in Bradfield. Andrews, who was no doubt a stranger to the area, accompanied Fearn as they walked towards Bradfield but as they neared Kirkedge on Onesmoor, he was shot by Fearn who only succeeded in wounding him. After stabbing him several times with a knife he finished the job with a hedging stake and robbed him of the watches in his possession. Fearn had however been seen with Andrews earlier in the day, and was soon arrested and taken to York for trial at the Assizes. He was found guilty and executed at Tyburn on 23rd July 1782. His body was brought back to Sheffield and hung in chains on a gibbet on Wadsley Common where it remained for fourteen years as a silent witness to his crime until the bones fell from the chains on Christmas Day. No trace remains as to the exact spot of the gibbet post but some accounts place it alongside Long Lane near to the car park entrance. Fearn's employer is reputed to have remarked that Fearn would come to a bad end and that he would die with his boots on. It is said, that Fearn, on the scaffold, immediately before he was executed, removed his boots in order to make him a liar.

LOW ASH FARM. High up on the hilltop overlooking the Loxley valley, this farm was once a Boarding School for young gentlemen. The school was established by a Mr. Linley in 1850 and continued for 30 years until his death in 1879. The 1861 Census records that John and Betsy Lindley, both 51 years of age, lived there with four daughters and 46 young gentleman boarders. Originally, there were two separate buildings but, in this century, a cottage was built joining the two buildings together. A feature inside the house is an old winding staircase leading to where the young gentlemen slept.

WORRALL HALL. Speculation exists as to whether the original Hall was built in 1720 by a family named Greaves. The building has a large circular stone plaque over the main doorway showing a shield containing crossed swords above the name Sarah, with the name John Greaves, 1720 below. Whether this is the same Sarah Greaves who was married to John Greaves and who, according to a report of the Charity Commissioners, donated £100 in November 1797, for the upkeep of Onesacre School, or their daughter, Sarah, who was born in 1712, is not known. In earlier years there was a cottage attached on one side which would appear to be much older than the rest and was probably built in the 17th Century, whilst on the opposite side, a larger stone built cottage was added in the 18th Century. When the buildings were falling into a poor state, some years ago, the new owner made major alterations and combined all three buildings into one residence.

Onesacre Hall after modernisation

Onesacre Hall before modernisation

Worrall Hall c1900

Worrall Hall Farm and Worrall Hall after alteration

Rural Cottage - Onesacre

Fox House - Top Road - Worrall, after modernisation

Oughtibridge Hospital Parade - 1913

Top Road and New Street, Oughtibridge, before demolition

*The Old School House - Wheel Lane
after modernisation.*

*The Old Post Office - Top Road - Oughtibridge.
Later Emma Cheetham's Fish & Chip Shop.*

Oughtibridge Station c1895

Jarville's Dam - Church Street - Oughtibridge

WORRALL HALL FARM. Adjoining Worrall Hall it is another of the oldest buildings in the village. An interesting feature of the farmhouse is the Insurance Plaque fixed to the front of the building. Farmed for many years by Mr Victor Codd until his death several years ago, it is no longer a working farm. In earlier years before the houses were built along Top Road, other farm buildings and the dairy known as Lund Farm were worked as part of Worrall Hall Farm.

FOX HOUSE. One of the oldest buildings in the area, it was once a coaching inn known as The Brown Cow. Situated on Top Road at Worrall, it dates back to the 17th Century. In recent years the cottage has been modernised but the unusual feature of being built on the Cruck principle has been retained and the original timbers still support the roof.

MIDDLEWOOD HALL. In earlier times it was the family home of the Fawcetts, Skelton's, Thorpes and later the Wilson's, all well known families in the district for many years. Originally a farmhouse, the Georgian style rectangular front was added by Mr. J.D.Skelton using local stone from the nearby quarries. The Hall is now in use as an hotel and is surrounded by 54 acres of parkland with a magnificent tree lined approach road through the woods. The two stone gateposts at the drive entrance facing the Old Toll Bar cottage near Hang Man, are surmounted by large stone carved urns. Local benefactors, the Skelton's were on the original Board of Governors when Worrall school was founded. My own family would appear to have a tragic connection with members of the Fawcett family who lived at Unstone Grange where, in 1920 my sister Winifred was whorled to death when her frock was caught in a revolving shaft of a corn grinding machine.

THE YEWS. Situated alongside Worrall Road, this large stone built house was erected by the Bramall's in the last century and the family lived there until the 1920's when their business ceased trading. For several years it has been used by The Trent Regional Hospital Board.

OUGHTIBRIDGE HALL. Among the oldest of the buildings in the area, it dates back to the sixteenth century and possibly earlier. One of the few buildings that existed in old Oughtibridge, near to Oughtibridge Green, up Oughtibridge Lane before the village became associated with the area known as Gate. Records refer to an old bed, dated 1640 which was said to have been made at Onesacre and which took a whole year to construct. Many people are reputed to have visited the Hall in order to see the ancient piece of furniture. An old manuscript describes a large oak tree that existed at the rear of the Hall which was eight yards round and twelve yards high and which was completely hollow. The outer rim was only a few inches thick, with a small hole at the bottom through which it was possible to creep in. It was finally destroyed when struck by lightening. In recent times it has ceased to be a farm and many of the buildings including a Cruck Barn have been modernised.

OUGHTIBRIDGE HALL FARM. Closely linked with the Hall, it dates back to 1530. An early photograph shows a decorated dray with tepee and Indians, ready to take part in the Oughtibridge Hospital Parade in 1911, an event which was important in the village in the early years of the century. Along with the Hall, the buildings have been renovated for housing and the old Crook Barn converted into a modern residence.

FORGE LANE COTTAGES. The cottages are amongst the oldest in the village with "The Lodge" dating back to the 17th century. Salmon fishing rights for the Don are shown on old Deeds. Nearby, at the entrance to Forge Lane, are the two gateposts which originally held large ornamental gates carrying the Wharncliffe Coat of Arms as the lane is believed to have formed the main entrance to the Wortley Estate.

BURTON FARM. Located a short distance below the Cemetery, this stone built farmhouse has a date stone over the door showing 1685. In the last century it was the home of Joseph Bramall who farmed there and later started ganister mining which led to the family becoming important in the district. The property has recently been modernised.

OUGHTIBRIDGE RAILWAY STATION. This Grade 2 listed building, made of gritstone, has been used for industrial purposes for several years following the closure of the station. Named by the railway as OUGHTY -BRIDGE, it dates back to 1845 as part of The Manchester, Sheffield and Lincolnshire Railway which later became The Great Central Railway and then The London & North Eastern Railway. In the 1930's it was still an important part of local life with many passengers using the station in order to get to Sheffield or Penistone. Mr. Sattin was the Station Master at that time and the position, along with that of Postmaster, Doctor and Schoolmaster, was one which commanded a great deal of respect in the village. I believe that Mr. Jack Robinson was a Linesman for a good number of years and Mr Brackenbury, a Signalman who served in the Signal Box, became an expert on the local wild life and birds, which he encouraged to visit his box.

I remember the many occasions when, on being late and, after running up Station Lane, the footbridge had to be crossed in one mad rush in order to catch the train which only stopped at the platform for a very short time. The sidings at the station were in frequent use, with wagons full of wood pulp waiting to be shunted down to the paper mill on their private line, whilst others carrying goods for the Oughtibridge Silica works would be waiting to be moved along the line that ran across Station Lane.

THE PENSIONERS HUT. This wooden structure stood for many years facing Coronation Park in Oughtibridge, until it was destroyed by fire. Originally used as The Oughtibridge Comrades Club, it was later the Headquarters of the local Pensioners Association. During the 1939/1945 war it was used as the local First Aid post. I remember being on duty there during the early part of the war when Oughtibridge became the target for German bombers. Members of the post were idly passing the time away playing table tennis, cards or reading, or just watching the huge rats which appeared frequently in the room, unaware that only a few hundred yards away a tragedy was unfolding. Eventually news arrived and everyone rushed to give what help they could. A single German plane had dropped a string of bombs across the valley, one of which had fallen on the row of cottages known as Bland Houses, near to Hang Man. Anyone reading the names on the War Memorial in Oughtibridge Parish Church may well wonder why the name of Woolhouse figures so prominently. Three members of the family were killed that night and it would appear that Mrs. Woolhouse saved her baby which was later brought up by other members of the family, by shielding it with her own body as she heard the sound of the approaching bomb. Several people did magnificent work and I believe one individual received an award for his efforts in rescuing the baby. The Woolhouse family were not the only people to suffer from the bombing. The end cottage was occupied by an elderly couple who, whenever the Air Raid sirens sounded, would take shelter under a stout deal table in the kitchen. With a courage that was typical of the times, whilst they were being rescued, they were insistent that their canary must be rescued as they had heard it singing and knew it was still alive.

JOHNNY WOODS ROW. Newcomers to the area may find it difficult to realise where these houses were. Situated adjacent to The Oughtibridge Co-operative Society on Langsett Road, the houses were actually built one on top of the other with the houses below being on the same level as Low Road. Nearby was a row of steep steps which allowed people to make a short cut to the Middlewood Forge and Tilt works on Low Road as well as to the stepping stones across the river Don for those who worked at the Silica bottom yard.

ZION TERRACE. Facing the Chapel on Top Road in Oughtibridge, the stone built row of houses and shops were demolished to make way for the Westnall House development. In the early part of the century, Miss Parkin's Millinery shop, The Office for the Overseer of the Poor, a Greengrocers shop, Parkin's Ironmongery shop, the Bus Yard, the Saddlers Shop and Stanley Arms all stood there.

CHERRYTREE ROW. Leading off Top Road in Oughtibridge and facing the Westnall House, this short row of cottages still remains.

BUTTON ROW. This tiny row of cottages at the side of Frank Hayward's shop on Langsett Road North, facing the Cock Inn car park were demolished along with Hayward's Butchers shop and the stone built houses on Top Road in the 1960's.

OFFICERS ROW. Situated up Church Street, above the Wesleyan Chapel, the stone built houses lay behind Zion Terrace until demolished to allow Westnall House to be built. Information regarding the connection between here and Hillsborough Barracks is hard to find but a century ago it was a common sight to see the horses from the Barracks being exercised in the area. Old census returns show that our family home was nearby in Glossop Row until my Grandfather moved to Fern Bank Terrace up Cockshutts Lane.

BARRACK'S ROW. Running parallel to Officers Row, a little higher up Church Street, the houses were part of the demolition that took place in the 1960's.

MITCHELL STREET. Further up Church Street, this small road was little more than a rough track that led up towards the Quarry. Near to Church Street was a small stone built building which I believe in earlier times was used as a Little Mester's workshop for the file cutting that many men in the village were engaged in.

Cottages - Towngate Road, Worrall.
Now demolished.

Grange Farm - Worrall, before demolition

Towngate - Worrall, before demolition

Well Cottage - Towngate Worrall

*The Old Post Office - Towngate Worrall.
Now demolished*

Manor Farm - Brightholmlee

Rag Harry at Wharncliffe Side

Pack Horse Bridge - Ewden, before removal to Glen Howe Park

The Worrall Coat of Arms
The Strines Inn

Blue Ball Inn - Warncliffe Side c 1910

Old Farmstead - Brightholmlee c 1910

Post Office - Wharncliffe Side

Main Road - Wharncliffe Side

WADSLEY - A NEIGHBOUR OF DISTINCTION

Several references have been made to the village of Wadsley and its association with Oughtibridge and Worrall over several centuries, so a brief look at its history will help us to appreciate how important it was in earlier times.

Hunter's "Hallamshire" has much to say about Wadsley and the surrounding area of Withala (Worrall) and Ughill which, in the Domesday Survey were shown as being held before the conquest by Aldene, a Saxon Lord. Later it became the seat of the Wadsley family, similar in rank to the De Ecclesalls and, like them held the estate in the name of a manor of the great baron at Sheffield castle, the De Furnivals, from which they adopted their heraldic insignia, adding three golden escallop shells for distinction. Sir Robert Wadsley had license to have divine service celebrated in the chapel or oratory constructed in his manor of Wadsley in 1409.

Earlier, in 1307, the King granted to Robert de Wadsley a market on Friday, at his manor at Rotherham, and a fair there for three days at the feast of St John the Baptist. The family of Wadsley had close association with the Everinghams of Stainborough when Margery, the daughter of Sir John Wadsley, Knight, around the time of Edward IVth, married Henry Everingham.

For many years there was a tradition among the inhabitants of Wadsley that the ancient owners of the hall were accustomed to entertain twelve men and their horses for twelve days at Christmas and at their departure each man was expected to stick a large pin or needle in the mantle tree. This may well have been a way of paying a rent in former times as it was common practice to pay rents in the form of thimbles, needles, thread and bodkins.

In 1561, the manors of Wadsley, Worrall and Wickersley were assigned to Sir Francis Leake who married one of the daughters of Robert Swyft, Esq, and Sir Francis later disposed of them to George, Earl of Shrewsbury who died siezed of them in 1590.

Over the years many notable families have lived in Wadsley, chief of which must surely be the Bamforths who lived there since the reign of Queen Elizabeth I. The Burton family appear to have been Lords of the Manor around 1789 when, by marriage it became the property of Ellen, the wife of George Bustard Greaves of Page Hall, Sheffield.

In 1812, John Fowler became tenant at the Hall and the family lived there for more than a century during which time the names of Fowler and Wadsley became well known in many parts of the world. He left behind a large family, one of which was Sir John Fowler, the engineer who designed the Pimlico Bridge, completed in 1860, the first railway bridge to cross the Thames and he also played an important part in many engineering projects throughout the world. His most important was the massive bridge over the Firth of Forth, over one and a half miles in length. Other members of the family also made their mark. William founded The Sheepbridge Iron and Steel Company, Henry was a civil engineer, Charles was an architect, Robert had a large practice as a solicitor in London whilst of the three daughters, one married a gentleman who became Government Superintendent of Railways in Australia, another married Captain Holmes of Norfolk and the other lived at Wadsley Hall with her father until her death in 1914. The freehold of the Hall was purchased by Sir John Fowler in 1884 and later passed to Sir John Edward Fowler, Bart, who was killed in action during the 1914-18 war. Belgium refugees occupied the Hall during the war and later the estate was broken up and sold and the Sutton estate built on part of the land.

In 1833-4 the Miss's Harrison of Sheffield built a house and Parsonage at Wadsley at a cost of £10,000 providing an endowment of £230 a year. Later, around 1840 Wadsley became a separate ecclesiastical district.

PLACE NAMES AND THEIR ORIGIN

OUGHTIBRIDGE. With kind permission of Mr. Jack Ambler, the Oughtibridge Church Historian, who's research into the name is acknowledged, the most likely origin of the name is as follows.

In the early years of the twelfth century a ford existed across the Don which was controlled by a man named Oughtred, who lived in a cottage nearby. When a bridge was built around 1150, it would seem natural for the bridge to be known as 'Oughtred's Bridge' or perhaps his nickname, Oughty's Bridge, in a similar way as Malin Stacey's Bridge, owner of a mill beside the bridge in the neighbouring Loxley valley and John Stock's Bridge, higher up the Don valley.

The community which sprang up around the bridge took its name from the bridge and gradually the 's' was dropped. With the arrival of the railway in the 1840's, it was known as 'Oughty Bridge', two separate words, for many years, although, in the wider area, the two words were merged into one, in a similar way to Stocksbridge. The Old English personal name Oughtred or Ughtred, of Anglo-Saxon origin, went out of fashion around the year 1200, when surnames were introduced, many of which were of Norman origin.

A legal document drawn up in 1161, known as 'The Convention of 1161', which defined an area of land on which the monks of Ecclesfield enjoyed Grazing Rights and which reached all the way from Ecclesfield to the banks of the Don, was signed by several witnesses who's land or property was involved. One of these signed himself 'Ralph, the Son of Oughtred'. To define the limit of the land in this direction, the name 'Ughtinabrigg' was used - Oughtred's Bridge.

Over the years changes have been made to the bridge. In 1730, Henry Hall of Oughtibridge and Benjamin Milnes of Worrall agreed to rebuild the bridge in stone. Modelled on the bridge at Deepcar, it was 33 yards long and 5ft wide. In the 1920's it was widened to its present width.

In more recent times there would appear to be a family named Oughtibridge as I remember a visitor from The United States making inquiring about the origin of his name. Only recently I met a young family who have moved into the district who are eager to find out more about their surname.

WORRALL. Believed to have originated from the Saxon word "HVIRFULL", meaning "top" which when linked to the word "FJALLSINS" meant "Top of the Hill", which could certainly apply to Worrall. In English, with a strong pronunciation of the letter "R", it would soon have become "Worrall" as we know it today. Old documents also referred to "WYRHALL", whilst in 1086, the Domesday Book linked the name "WITHALA" with Wadsley and Ughill. This was thought by many to refer to Worrall.

BOGGARD LANE. Old maps show this as more of an important thoroughfare than the main road from Worrall to Oughtibridge. Perhaps, when horse drawn carts and wagons were used to transport the stone from the many quarries in the area, or farmers at the nearby farms passed with their drays, found that the animals were startled or "boggled" as if by some spectre or goblin as they passed along the road, it became known by that name. This derives from the word "bogle", the Northern form of which was "boggard".

COCKSHUTTS LANE. Around one hundred years ago some documents referred to this as "Cock Chute Lane." At that time the road was a steep narrow track that required the help of the "Cock" horse to pull a cart or dray up the steep hillside. The name may well have originated from the Cockshutt family as the name of James Cockshutt Esq. is mentioned as an arbiter in a dispute between George Grayson and John Kenyon in 1803 when Kenyon had increased the height of the weir on the Don causing the river to back up and stall the corn mill water wheel.

THE DELFS. High up on the hillside above the hamlet of Hill Top, this area of woodland has been extensively quarried which has left the hillside scarred with sheer cliff faces. The pathways wind their way through the rock strewn ground towards Tinker Brook with a mixture of wild vegetation, untouched for years, all around. I remember seeing a grass snake there, many years ago. One rock face still has a cave several feet square in which a hermit once lived. He became known locally as Dance David as, on his visits to the village, he would be followed by children calling out for him to dance. He would often oblige by giving a jump into the air and kicking his heels together. Alternative spellings of delves, delphs are sometimes used, but all would appear to mean excavations, a drain or ditch, which would certainly apply.

THE DUN COW AND CALF. High up on Onesmoor with its wonderful panoramic view stretching in all directions, near to the aerial masts of the University, one can still find the two stones, one larger than the other, that are boundary markers denoting the extent of ownership of land. The dictionary lists Dun-cow as shagreen, a granular leather made from horses or asses skin, covered in small nodules. It would be interesting to know the connection.

VILLAGE CRICKET

As long ago as the middle of the nineteenth century when industry often demanded that employees worked long hours, sport still formed an important part of village life. Hound trailing created a good deal of interest with much hard earned money changing hands as bets were accepted as to which dog would win. The desire to hit something as far as possible, may have led to the old game of Knurr and Spell which was played wherever a large open space could be found. The small round "Potty" which was often hit a great distance, can frequently be found by the gardener when digging the garden. I remember, as a small boy, watching a game in The Myers, about 1929, and as recently as 1992 two men were seen playing in a field at the top of Jaw Bone hill, near Stephen Lane.

The same desire to hit a moving object may well have encouraged local men to play the game of cricket, as early records show that the game was being played in Oughtibridge as long ago as 1874. Oughtibridge Church Cricket Club were playing in a field up Birtin Lane, immediately below the Cemetery. The Zion Cricket Club was also in existence, playing their games in a field above "The Planting", alongside Jossey Lane.

The two clubs continued in existence until 1919 when they amalgamated to form Oughtibridge Cricket Club which continues to play cricket in The South Riding League up to the present time. The ground known as The Berrying Close, or by some as The Bedding Close, alongside Station Road, was donated to the village in 1921 by Oughtibridge Silica Firebrick Company Limited. as a War Memorial to the fallen who died in the 1914 - 1918 war.

The present day club can only envy the participation and support given in those early days by so many of the local prominent personalities. The names of the Presidents and Patrons are like a 'Who's Who' of the history of the village and surrounding district, with many of the local industrialists, doctors and others, anxious to be associated with the sport. The Dixon's were represented by Mr. Joseph Dixon and Mr.L.B.Dixon, Oughtibridge Silica Firebrick Company by Mr. F.H. Brooke and Wardlow's Steel Works by Mr. M Wardlow. Others included Messrs F.M.Bramall, E.Halstead, P.J.Turner and the local Headmaster, Mr. J.P.Barratt. and the vicar, The Rev W.G.Largie, with Dr. Hall, Dr. Marsh and Dr. Wyndham, the local Doctors also lending their patronage. Dr. Hall was not strictly a local as he lived in the large house at the bottom of Marlcliffe Road, at Wadsley, but he hired a room in a house along Station Lane, just above the park, as a surgery.

In 1906, the Church team played in the Norton and District League but it was not until 1914 that they achieved their first success by winning the championship. Extracts from the Minutes of the Church Cricket Club meetings, which were held in the

Wesleyan Reform schoolroom, make interesting reading. March.19 .1906. President. Alderman C.Bramall, Secretary, J.Tonks, Treasurer, W.H.Lister. February 11, 1913. Agreed that we have a concert and have Pierrots and Mr. S.E.Lenthall be asked to be chairman. September 15, 1914. After 40 years in existence, Oughtibridge Cricket Club gained first honours by winning the Championship of the Norton and District League. Proposed we have 14 medals and delegates be allowed 2s-6p for purchase. Proposed we have a coffee supper and ask Mr. Thorpe to present medals and Rev G.W.Largie to be Chairman. October 28.1914. Proposed that we have a wagonette to fetch Cup and medals on November 2nd. October 15,1915. That we try and get as many as possible to help to level the ground somewhat, by removing some of the soil from the top side to the bottom. Undated 1916. The Season 1916 was a record for the Oughtibridge Church Cricket Club. It was the first season in the Hallamshire League and they carried off the Championship, not even dropping a single point. October 13, 1919. Decided to call another meeting and invite Zion members with a view to amalgamation. October 13, 1922. Proposed we have a rabbit pie supper and concert, some Monday night after Flag presentation in Sheffield. November 15, 1922. The season of 1922 has been the best ever experienced since cricket was first played at Oughtibridge and it must be over fifty years ago. The first eleven have won the "B" Division of the Hallamshire League carrying with it a beautiful Flag and also promotion to the first division. The second team have also won their division and Flag. A real good performance. The third team have finished 2nd in the Chapeltown League, only being defeated by one point. The team defeated Barnes Green by dismissing them for one run. T.Thomas, 7 wickets for 0 runs and A.Glossop, 3 wickets for 1 run. February 25. 1932. That some form of memorial be initiated to the late Ronnie Walters and it was decided this should take some form of a cup to be bought by the club and to be known as "The Ronnie Walters Cup". This cup is still awarded annually to the winners of the "D" Division of the Sheffield Cricket League.

Since 1921 when the ground was presented to the village, cricket and football have continued to be played there up to the present time. For several years two tennis courts were situated on the site where the pavilion now stands, but in 1935, when serious flooding took place, the courts were washed away. In those days the club relied heavily on "Gate" receipts for its income and Tommy Dransfield, or "Limpy Tommy" as he was affectionately known because of the iron on one shoe, made sure that everyone paid to watch the game.

Any account of cricket in Oughtibridge would not be complete without mention of some of the names of players who left their mark on the game locally. The name of Glossop must rank high in the list, which is not surprising as no less than seven brothers all played for the village club, with as many as five playing in the same side on several occasions. The eldest was Walter, better known as "Tal" who for many years was captain at both football, where he played at inside left, and cricket, where he was stumper and opening bat. He played football until he was 38 but went on to play cricket until he was 50 years of age. His memories of cricket in the early 1900's give a vivid picture of how dedicated one had to be in order to play the game. Ernest Glossop, when ninety years of age, still enjoyed relating stories about the men and the games played so many decades ago. An away match at White Lane, Chapeltown, often meant a long walk to get there, whilst for an away fixture at Hathersage, it was necessary to hire old Ely Morton's wagonette which could seat up to 22 passengers and required two horses to pull it. It needed a 10 o'clock start in order to get there for 3 p.m. and it was late in the evening when they arrived back at Oughtibridge after refreshment at one or two of the local hostelries.

Two other brothers served the club with distinction for many years. John and Tommy Roberts were both very useful with the bat, so much so that it was said that Tommy could have played for Yorkshire. Just what his reaction was in 1925, when the Captain, Walter Glossop, in what he described as "the Grandest match he had ever seen", declared, when Oughtibridge had scored 240 for 5 wickets against Hallam and Tommy Roberts was 93 Not Out.

It is not possible to mention all the players who, in the past, made Oughtibridge worthy opponents for any other team in the surrounding district, but a few who come to mind include the two Minnis's, Ronnie Walters, Raymond Gott, and his two sons, John and Barry who sadly, whilst batting for Whitley Hall against his old club, Oughtibridge, collapsed and died, the George Morton's, father and son, Cyril Ball, Lol Buet, Denis Lister, the Nornables- Alf and Doug and Roy Dennis, who's brother -in-law was Len Hutton, and Edgar Sheldon.

VILLAGE FOOTBALL

Like the game of cricket, football was first played in the last century when the lack of transport meant that most games were against other teams in close proximity, although my father recounted a similar story to the cricketers, of matches against Hathersage which required a horse drawn wagonette to get there.

Although the village team have always been noted for their high standard of football, it would seem that the height of their achievement was early in the century, in the season 1919 - 1920 when Oughtibridge won the Junior Challenge Cup and the Sheffield Minor League championship. The Cup Final was played at Bramall Lane when they beat Swallownest 5-1 and went on to win the Minor League by beating Greasbrough 2-1. Memories of that period were vividly recaptured by Mr. Fred Howson, an old Oughtibridge resident who was an ardent supporter and travelled everywhere with the team. He recalled the many fine players who proudly wore the teams colours, several of whom were all round sportsmen as they also played in the village cricket team, Tom and John Roberts, Jack Hammerton, who had played with Barnsley and Rotherham, Collet, who joined Arsenal, and Dick Coldwell, who played for Sheffield Wednesday. The captain, "Tal" Glossop, who was also the captain of the cricket team, was tall and well built and had a fine footballing relationship with Bernard Cooke, better known amongst the footballing fraternity as "Johnny Holt" due to his style and appearance resembling that of the Everton star of years ago. Another member of that great team was Lol Buet, who played at centre-half. He played as an amateur for both Sheffield Wednesday and Derby County as well as a professional for Rotherham Town and continued playing for Oughtibridge until well past his 40th birthday.

As a reminder of those far off days, a photograph of the Cup winning side taken at Bramall Lane, is displayed in the Oughtibridge War Memorial Sports Club and pictured in the photograph are (from left to right), Standing, H.Helliwell (Secretary), A. Edwards, C.Lenthall, L. Haywood, J. White, T. Woodhead, (Uncle of Denis Woodhead, who played for Sheffield Wednesday for many years), and L. Buet. Seated: B. Cooke, G. Siddall, Glossop, W. Glossop, Albert Peace and J.Ridgewell, (Trainer).

Another period which is still remembered by a few older residents was climaxed when, in 1937, the village team playing in The Friendlies League, won every league match and were awarded the Green'un Ball. To celebrate, a dance was held in the Parish Hall when Jack Smith, a local goalkeeper of renown, presented badges to the players. The team, as far as I can ascertain was made up of the following; Ray Gott, Frank Grayson, George Morton, Alec Guest, Edwin Wood, Alf Nornable, Geoff Sattin, Harold Parkin, George Wilkinson, Doug Nornable and Machin, who's Christian name cannot be recalled. The season ended less satisfactorily when, playing in the final of the A.J.Sanders trophy, the team was beaten 1-0 by Woodseats Methodists, Ray Gott missing a penalty.

Earlier years also had their personalities. As far back as 1895 when the village team played in Bridge Field, now Coronation Park, Jack Hudson, formally a professional with both Sheffield Wednesday and United, was an international and played for Oughtibridge after his professional days were over.

THE VILLAGE BAND

For over a century, very few events have taken place in the area without the village band being involved, and for many years it has been a mainstay of village life.

Details of when and where the band was formed are not recorded but, thanks to the information provided by the late Mr. Clifford Grace who lived at Wharncliffe Side and who, for over sixty years was actively associated with the band, much of its history is known.

Around 1890, six well known local residents each put twenty-five pounds into the kitty and with the one hundred and fifty pounds, bought instruments and equipment. These benefactors were George Fairest, Licensee of the Station Inn, William Hill, a farmer on Jawbone Hill, Ben Lawton, a joiner at Oughtibridge Silica Firebrick Company Ltd., James Bennett, Blacksmith, Edwin Halstead, General Manager at the Silica Works and Charles Lenthall, General Manager of S & C Wardlow Ltd., who's premises were up Station Lane, above the railway line.

In the early years when little transport existed, the band played mainly at local events, as an engagement at Grenoside or Stocksbridge entailed a long walk carrying heavy instruments. Christmas was a tiring time, with the band starting in the early hours of Christmas Day and Boxing Day, playing carols at the outlying farms and Public Houses before returning home late in the day. Mr. Grace recalled how, as a boy he was playing in the band at Haigenfield when the owner, Mr. Josiah Kaye, was not very impressed with the cornet he was playing and gave him an old instrument he had in the house. Years later, when buying a new instrument, the Company took the instrument in part-exchange and gave him five pounds as well. The old cornet was a collectors piece and became part of the firm's museum.

Over the years, many members of the same families have been associated with the band. William Mallinson and his six sons were members, as were the Robinson brothers, Ernest and Irvine, the Brearley brothers, Alonza and Bill. George Howson and his son Frank, the Cooper's, Fred, Frank and Irvine and the Croft's Arthur, Stan and Herbert, who were later joined by cousin Job and his son Robert. The four members of the Wright family, Billy, Ronnie, Bernard and Harold who later emigrated to Australia, as did the Wilson's, Edward and Thomas. No account of the history of the band would be complete without mention of those present members who after years of devoted and dedicated service, still strive to maintain the high standards achieved over the years. Chief among these must surely be the Secretary, Mr Tom Holmes.

The band has seen several changes to its name. At one time it was known as The Don Valley Brass Band and later became The Oughtibridge and District Silver Prize Band until it took its present name of Oughtibridge Band.

Oughtibridge Band

PASTIMES

Towards the end of the last century, and for the first three decades of the 20th century when the lack of transport meant that people tended to make their own enjoyment, local organisations flourished and did much to make life in the villages more bearable. Mention has already been made of the dancing that took place in Oughtibridge above Hayward's shop and at the rear of the Station Inn, some one hundred years ago. In later years, dances were held in the Parish Hall, which became a much more formal affair, with ladies in Evening Dress and gentlemen in Dinner Jackets or Tails.

Gilbert and Sullivan Operettas were regularly produced in the Wesleyan Reform School room. I remember our music stool was always full of copies of the Pirates of Penzance, The Mikado, The Gondoliers and many others, after my two sisters had taken part in the productions.

The village Horticultural Society thrived for many years. The annual show was held in the Zion schoolroom and I have vivid memories of the morning of the Show when I had the job of helping to take my Grandfather's exhibits from his allotment on The Planting and woe betide me if I damaged the single rose exhibit which had been carefully nurtured under its specially made glass cover. The pensioners bungalows now stand on the site of the allotments at Crag View.

Day trips were the most that people could afford and these would often be by wagonette to Honley or, in later years, by coach to Cleethorpes or Skegness. Evening trips to Bridlington by rail became possible, as more and more people recovered from the hard times following the depression in the 1920's.

Sunday evening would find courting couples and small groups of young men and women taking a stroll along "The Monkey Rack", adjacent to the Middlewood Tavern. This may seem tame by today's standard, but many a boy met his future wife after a stroll there.

The children also had their pastimes. With few distractions from Radio and later, Television, they were often left to their own invention. Games of "Relievo" would extend over quite a distance, whilst the "Den", solidly built from stone, by the older boys from Crag View, was sited on a narrow strip of land immediately above a rock cliff face along Usher Wood. On one occasion, after an argument amongst the boys, one parent, complete with striking hammer, found that it was too solidly built for him to demolish.

Another favourite place for children to play was the clay mine in The Myers. There were two entrances to the drift mines which had tramways on which the trucks or

"Corves" were pushed. After leaving the mine, the truck had to travel down a pronounced slope which had a sharp bend before travelling some fifty yards to the loading chute above Usher Wood. Here the axles of the truck passed over a metal fork which allowed it to be upturned to let the clay drop down the chute. What a thrill it was to use a piece of cardboard as a seat whilst plummeting down the chute. A ride on a truck was a hair raising event and often ended with clothes and legs covered in axle grease. This could result in two good hidings, one for playing in the pit and the other for getting covered in grease. Another game played in the pit, often ended in tears and bruises. Two teams would be chosen and forts built by criss-crossing the timbers used for lining the sides of the drift mines. Bark from the large piles of pit props was collected for ammunition, and battle began with boys bobbing up above the parapet and quickly throwing at the enemy in the opposing fort.

Dark Autumn evenings were an ideal time for games of mischief. These would include the "Bullroar", a rather dangerous prank which entailed inserting newspaper into the end of the cast iron drainpipe and igniting it. The resulting roar was at times quite dramatic although the risk of setting fire to the wooden spouting must have been quite high. Other favourite pranks of the children which was guaranteed to get neighbours very cross, was to tie the handles of the doors together with strong rope, knock on both doors and watch the resulting tug-of-war from a safe distance. Another was to pin buttons tied on to black cotton on to a window frame and gently pull on the cotton from some distance away to cause an irritating rattle on the glass.

Many of the children's games of years ago have survived with very little change. Hopscotch, skipping, ball games and hide and seek still have their annual period of activity but others have been lost with the passing years. Rarely now do we see children playing marbles, whip and top or running with a metal hoop and hook or playing tip-stick. In the same way that adults playing Knurr and Spell would endeavour to hit a small round 'potty' as far as possible, this game required a round piece of wood some two inches long, pointed at both ends, to be 'tipped' into the air with a stick and then hit as far as possible.

The row of substantial trees known as The Planting, near to Crag View Crescent, was a favourite place for many to play. Around 1930, a trapeze was built between two of the trees and had ropes over fifteen feet long. These allowed the trapeze to be used in two ways, one, by climbing a little way up the tree trunk and catching the bar with one hand, before releasing the grip on the tree and flying through the air. The second demanded more courage and no little skill, for it entailed climbing higher into the tree and assuming a crouch position, ready to catch the trapeze when it was thrown. The act of swinging from the tree took a great deal of determination but was finally halted when one boy was being persuaded, against his better judgment, to try the greater height. His grip on the trapeze bar was not sufficient to hold him and he crashed to the ground, breaking his arm.

Summer holidays would find children swimming in the Don in Beely Wood at a strip of smooth water known as "The Homes" or towards Wharncliffe Side, beyond what was known as the "Black Pit" in the "Sandy Bed".

The coming of the cinema had a major impact on the local community which relied on Hillsborough with its three cinemas, The Kinema, The Park Cinema and the Phoenix for entertainment. Public transport had become established and people from Oughtibridge would travel by bus to the terminus at Middlewood and then either walk or catch the tram for the rest of the journey. The site of the bus terminus can still be seen where the gap in the wall exists, some 50 yards from Terminus Garage at Middlewood. Local musicians, including Mr. Harry Minnis provided musical accompaniment in the days of the silent films and the Saturday morning "Two penny Rush" would guarantee there would be a full house of screaming noisy children, especially when the heroine lay fast on the railway line as the express train rushed towards her, only for the film to end and the children urged to watch the next instalment to find out if she was rescued. People had their own loyalties as to which cinema they attended. I must admit to a preference for the Kinema House on Proctor Place with its twice nightly shows and queues right around the cinema. Saturday night was not complete without a visit to the Sarsaparilla shop facing Proctor Place along Middlewood Road. The Phoenix cinema, opposite the entrance to Hillsborough Barracks, was a favourite with courting couples and there was always a rush for the two person seats on the balcony which was only a raised area a few feet higher than the Stalls. The cinema had more than its fair share of cowboy films and it was a standing joke that after the last show on the Saturday, all the horse dirt had to be swept out ready for the following week. A night at the cinema would usually include two main films, forthcoming attractions and of course the latest news brought to you by Gaumont British News or Pathe News. In those days it was the practice to change the films being shown at least twice a week whilst in the surrounding villages it was commonplace for a mobile cinema to visit the local village hall and put on a film show.

Some of my fondest memories are of a sporting nature when, on being taken to Bramall Lane by Mother and Father to watch Yorkshire play at cricket, I was able to peer through the Pavilion window at some of the great players of the past. Even now a feeling of nostalgia exists at the thought of watching Herbert Sutcliffe, Hedley Verity, Bill Bowes, Maurice Leyland and other great players preparing to go out and do battle against Lancashire in front of a 20,000 crowd. In those days Bramall Lane was reknowned for its knowledgeable crowd and for the wit that was bandid around the ground. On one occasion Yorkshire were struggling and Norman Yardley was finding it difficult to score runs. One wag in the crowd yelled out advice " Tha supposed to hit t' ball wi' t'bat", where-upon another voice from the other side of the ground called out, "Thee shut tha gob. What's tha know abart it". Back came the reply, "Thee shut tha gob. ' I'm talking te Fitter not 'is oily rag"

THE CHORES OF DAYS GONE BY

Trimming wicks, cleaning and polishing the oil lamps.
Cleaning out the fireplace and carrying in the wood and coal.
Blackleading the Yorkshire range.
Monday Washday.
Boiling water. Dollying clothes. Mangling.
Tuesday ironing.
Baking.
Making spills.
Cutting and threading newspapers for the toilet.
Cutting up cloth and pegging rugs.
Changing gas mantles.
Cutting the lawn with hand held shears.
Picking Raspberries and Blackcurrants.
Using an outside toilet.
Sitting on a horse hair sofa in short trousers.

YESTERDAY'S TREATS

Bread and Dripping.
Bread and Sugar.
HP Sauce on bread.
Slices of apple, covered in sugar and left overnight between saucers,
ready to be eaten on awakening.
Being allowed to stay up for the Carollers at Mid-night on Christmas Day.
New clothes at Whitsuntide.
A Pennypop from Bankwell Spring.
A halfpenny to buy sweets.
A Hot Cross Bun at Easter.
Riding on a Hay cart.
A day trip to Honley.
An evening rail trip to the coast.
Choir trips.
Nettle Beer.
Dandelion and Burdock.